T0114719

From Karma to Christ

MY JOURNEY FROM RELIGION TO RELATIONSHIP

Chhali Kharel Bista

WESTBOW
PRESS®
A DIVISION OF THOMAS NELSON
& ZONDERVAN

WestBow Press books may be ordered through booksellers or by contacting:

WestBow Press
A Division of Thomas Nelson & Zondervan
1663 Liberty Drive
Bloomington, IN 47403
www.westbowpress.com
844-714-3454

ISBN: 978-1-6642-9080-8 (sc)
ISBN: 978-1-6642-9079-2 (e)

Print information available on the last page.

WestBow Press rev. date: 03/09/2023

DEDICATION

I want to dedicate this book to my readers, especially the younger generation, who may not have experienced struggling with identity and hopelessness as a displaced citizen. When you have adequate food, shelter, both parents, and an identity, it is difficult to imagine life without them.

It is also hard, then, to understand what a blessing it is to have an "eternal" identity and a relationship with the God who created the universe, our eternal Father, who knows each of us by name. I encourage readers to see the real truth for, "The Truth shall set you free" (John 8:32).

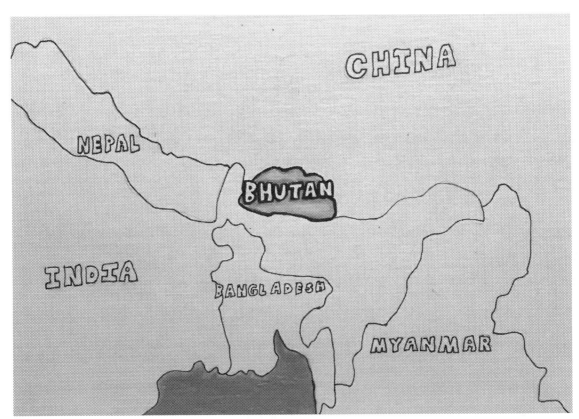

Born in Bhutan, lived in a refugee camp in Nepal for 18 years, and came to America.

FROM KARMA TO CHRIST
MY JOURNEY FROM RELIGION
TO RELATIONSHIP

HISTORY OF BHUTAN

Bhutan has a very interesting and complicated history. There is not a lot known about it compared to other countries in the world. It is a country that lies between China and India. It is part of the Himalayan Mountain range. It is called the land of the Thunder Dragon. Druk means "Dragon", pas means "people". Drukpa are the dragon people. Buddhist priest literature and chronicles began the recorded history of Bhutan. Tibetan migration to Bhutan brought a new culture and established a fresh, new reimagined Bhutan with democratic leanings.

The first king of Bhutan was Ugyen Wangchuk who reigned from 1907-1926. The second king was his son, Jigme Wangchuk, who reigned from 1926-1952. The third king, Jigme Jorje Wangchuk, who reigned from 1952-1972, was followed by the fourth king, Jigme Singe Wangchuk, from 1972-2006. The fifth and final king, who currently reigns, is Jingme Khesar Namgyal Wangchuk (2006-present).

The national language is Dzongkha. Bhutanese political development was heavily influenced by religious history. Because of the constant threat of invasion from Tibet, Bhutan brought together the most powerful Bhutanese families called the Drukyal in one place to prevent invasion from Tibet. India also sent a group of people from several villages to Bhutan to contribute to the new culture.

LIFE IN BHUTAN

I was born in 1979 (exact date is unknown) at home on the outskirts of the jungle at the base of the Himalayan Mountain Range in Bhutan. Our home didn't have electricity or running water or access to any type of market or medical facilities close by. Six months after I was born my father died, leaving my mom a widow with two daughters. We did have maternal and paternal uncles and a large family network for support. Even though we didn't have modern conveniences, we had food aplenty due to the farming nature of Bhutan. We had oil, orchards full of oranges, pomegranates, plums, peaches, pears and more available to us. We could barter with other families for milk and cheese. Families made money by selling their crops, mainly oranges, beans and cardamon. Life was hard but relatively secure and predictable. We had orchards to pick fruit from and sell, we had goats for meat and to sell. We kept sheep for meat and wool. Cows and oxen were kept for milk, butter and cheese and for religious purposes. Bhutan is 90% agriculture. Everyone farmed multiple things as a way of life.

We were at the bottom of the Himalayan mountains and our weather was usually moderate. Because we were in a mountain range we walked up and down hilly terrain along the edge of the jungle. A village would have approximately 10 or 11 family homes. To go to another village was a short 15-minute walk on the outskirts of the jungle. For transportation we used our feet and horses.

This house is similar to my home in Bhutan surrounded by orchards.

A BIT ABOUT MY FAMILY HISTORY IN THE BHUTANESE-NEPALI CULTURE

My mom and dad were products of the extreme cultural practices of the day. My father had a wife and a daughter. Females were not highly valued in those times and were often less valuable in the eyes of the culture than a cow. My father "needed" a son for funeral practices when he would die as per Hindu rules. He sent his first wife (my stepmom) to find him another younger wife that could potentially give him a son. This is how my mom came into the picture. She was 13 years old and, as the practice was at this time, a girl could be engaged and promised to a man at a young age and then would be given to him in marriage after she became able to produce children. My stepmom approached my grandparents to ask for my mom's hand in marriage for my father which broke her heart, but she had no choice in the matter and had to perform this duty. I can't imagine how heartbreaking this was for my stepmom and my sister Dambari.

My mom was young and innocent with little to no education, as were all women at that time. She spent her days watching many head of cattle in the jungle in a primitive sort of world. She was plucked from this simple, innocent life (when she was able to have babies) and plopped into a new entangled marriage with an already married man who was twice her age. As time went by, my mom and stepmom lived in separate homes and my dad would go back and forth between them. My mom ended up having three daughters; the first dying at 7 months and the next two being my oldest sister and then me. We all were born at home. My mom worked on the farm until she was ready to deliver. So my dad ended up with three daughters and no sons. My stepmom treated my mom like a daughter and was kind and loving and was also this way to my sister and me and still to this very day. What started out as a kind of curse has blossomed into a great blessing. My older sister Tika was my dearest teacher and role model as a child.

Before he could try for a son, my dad unfortunately died a quick and unexpected death. Because we had no access to a hospital for making a diagnosis or any type of care beyond a general checkup, my dad suffered with something serious with symptoms of weight loss, fever and rectal bleeding. The day before he died he was out deer hunting with friends and came home, threw up blood and then passed away quickly. I was six months old when this happened and my sister was only three and a half years old. My mom was only in her early twenties and now was a young widow. So my mom and stepmom became very close amid this disaster and loss and worked together from there on out to raise their children and care for them. All five of us were worthless females in the world's eyes but God had a purpose for us then as He still does today.

WHY I AM CALLED BHUTANESE-NEPALI

I was born in Bhutan during the kingship of Jigme Singe Wangchuk. Because Bhutan needed people to come to the country to help populate and develop it into a new country, some Nepali were invited to come, as well, to populate the lowlands of southern Bhutan in the mid to late 19th century. My grandmother, who would be 105 if she were still alive, had three babies when she moved to Bhutan. She and my grandpa moved in approximately 1943. They served the country along with the other Nepalese in building the country from the ground up in construction and agricultural development. Bhutanese citizens of Nepali origin (people of the south) are called Lhotshampas.

My mom and dad were born in Bhutan, but spoke Nepali and practiced Hinduism instead of Buddhism. Thus, we are called Bhutanese-Nepali because our ancestors are Nepali from Nepal, but because of the migration to Bhutan we are still Nepali by culture but born in Bhutan. So we are both Bhutanese and Nepali just like the Israelites who were born in Egypt. The Nepali population grew so much by the 1990s that the Bhutan king and the Druk majority became concerned like the Pharoah in Egypt, that they could threaten the majority position.

LHOTSHAMPAS BETRAYAL

The Nepali people lived peacefully with all people groups and worked very hard in constructing the country and growing crops. Many were hard-working contributors who made this country beautiful. They were so willing and worked so hard because they were building a future in this new country for their children and generations to come. However, a campaign from the government called "One Country, One People" was developed to "unify" the country culturally. Bhutan then required all citizens to dress in the Drukpa tradition, practice Buddhism only, and use the same language regardless of their native language. These new changes negatively impacted the Lhotshampa people. They had been invited to come to this country to live according to their own cultural ideas and were now being stripped of this right. Further, human rights violations started to emerge. Textbooks were burned, teachers fired, and the Nepali language was forbidden to be spoken in school or in public. Additionally, the Bhutan government cracked down on the Lhotshampa people with regard to proving their citizenship. They practiced unrealistic and stringent strategies even when proof of citizenship documentation was given. Eventually, the King chose only a certain number of people to stay in the country following the "One Country, One People" rules and the rest were uninvited to stay in the country and required to leave.

USED UP AND DISCARDED

We got a letter from the government giving us three days to leave the country. We had no time to sell anything we had worked so hard for. Our livestock, crops, fruits and farm had to be abandoned. We were shocked and dismayed. We had rice, wheat, beans and other items stored in the barn that we couldn't take with us. We also hid the tool box and farm tools into a cave thinking we would be coming back. We had to untie and release the livestock. We had to turn our backs on everything that we owned and start walking. I was 11 years old and I packed two pairs of clothes and a bit of food for the unknown journey. Before we left, we gathered our three families and my grandmother wailed and cried. She expressed her anguish of being brought here from nothing, with the promise of new starts and citizenship, and now being tossed away like garbage after 48 years of hard work, acquiring wealth and prosperity. To be broken again and losing the legacy and heritage she had given her life to build for her family shattered her dreams and the dreams of both sets of grandparents with this injustice. My uncles, aunts, and cousins all wept. We had all worked hard and had become wealthy and prosperous and were so hopeful for the future of their families. Now all we had were little backpacks and marched through the villages, crossing the river to reach the place to connect with the industrial type truck that would haul us off to who knows where like many bags of garbage to be tossed away. We had a sweet pet, a dog named Bhutto, that followed us all the way to the truck and she cried and cried when we were loaded.

There were so many of us crammed into this industrial vehicle that there was standing room only. As we traveled down the mountain, we were tossed back and forth, bumping into each other and being tossed around. I was so motion sick that I threw up to the point that I was puking blood. The truck traveled to the other side of the border into India and dumped us off with so many other castoffs. We immediately started collecting stones to make an open-fire oven to cook our food using dirty river water. We made mats from hay to sleep on and we drank from a small stream. After three days a bus came and drove us to a refugee camp in Nepal by the bank of the Maidhar river.

INITIAL REFUGEE CAMP

Because of disputes over citizenship and political unrest, many Bhutanese Nepali people were consider illegal aliens and were sent out of the country to refugee camps in 1991. One hundred thousand people were forced to exit Bhutan and go to Nepal where they originated. In Nepal, life was much more difficult and poverty was the tone of life there. Life in the refugee camp was ugly and scary and difficult for many reasons. The first 7 months we had to live on the bank of Maidhar River. It was called the Maidhar River Camp. When we first arrived, we had no water, no toilet facilities and no electricity. We had no access to medical care. Our home was open to the elements like a makeshift tent that wasn't waterproof. We slept on the muddy floor on blankets huddled in a small, crowded space. Basically, the sky was our roof, the horizon was our wall and the earth was our floor. We really felt hopeless and in despair; hungry, scared and unsure of our future. Life did improve some after the first few months when we received more food and a small amount of medical supplies. A stench hung in the air from poor sanitation and burning bodies on the river bank. One hundred people per day died and their bodies were burned and ashes dumped into the river, polluting it. Dysentery, fever and malnutrition were the main causes of death at this time. This is the backdrop of my life during my 12th year.

Seven months after arriving in this camp, different worldwide agencies came to divide this huge camp into 7 smaller camps in different locations in the eastern part of Nepal. Our family was assigned to the largest refugee camp, called Beldangi II. The weather was much better there as we were now on the edge of the forest. We didn't have private toilet facilities until three months later so we walked into the jungle with water to use the bathroom. We finally got a toilet to share with another hut.

Our food supply consisted of rice, lentils, oil, salt, sugar and sometimes root vegetables which were not fresh. For water we had one tap for 100 people and we had to fetch the water in a bucket, waiting in line for a long time, twice a day. Food was never enough to last 15 days so we were always hungry. When we moved to our new place, we were given 20 bamboo trees to erect a house with plastic for a roof; we made bricks out of mud for the walls and our floors were dirt. When storms came, the roof was always a worry since we thought it would blow off.

If tree branches fell, they could not be stopped by the plastic. Many people died from falling branches and trees, knocking the huts down. Others were trampled by elephants. We literally lived in the jungle with cobras, tigers, spiders, cockroaches and bedbugs. Lice were prevalent, as well, because we didn't have enough water to stay clean. Because we didn't have a man in our home, our house was not as sturdy as it could have been had we had help to make it strong, even though people did help us. We had a makeshift kitchen in our "house" in which we cooked over an open fire, causing fires that burned people's homes. People died because of the inherent danger of open fire cooking in a small space made of bamboo.

Cooking inside the hut with charcoal and firewood

Initial refugee camp picture in Maidhar by the riverbank.

From left to right: myself, my mother Indra and sister Tika
Removing stones and chaff from the rice provided by the United Nations.
In Beldangi Camp, 2000

SCHOOL IN THE REFUGEE CAMP IN NEPAL

For the first two years in the refugee camp, we attended school in the shade of trees. We sat on a burlap sack which we brought and when the sun moved, we moved with it to stay in the shade. We didn't have enough school supplies at this time so we shared books in rotation and the teacher's materials were blackboard and chalk. For writing utensils, we had a refillable ink pen that would leak all over our hands and it would smear on the paper. We would wash the paper off and put it in the sun to dry and reuse it once again. We practiced our math and writing on it. Our ankles were calloused from the roughness of the sacks as we sat on them cross-legged all day long. A school was erected with bamboo sticks, a thatch roof and the same old mud floor. A few more years later we finally got desks and benches. We never had electronics or lab materials; we spent our time memorizing facts about science and history. We had no food or snacks or meals at the school. We could just get water from a faucet and put it in our hands. Unfortunately, if we didn't have our memorization done well or if anyone was ever naughty at all, the teachers would beat us. It was acceptable in this country and others around us to beat children even if they were not your own. Fortunately for me I was a top student, always first or second in my class.

There were 45 or 50 students in my class, all in the same grade. School was available from preschool to grade 10 only in the camp. After grade 10 we could go to high school for Grades 11 and 12 and we could choose what to focus on for future college courses. I chose to focus on science and math. Scholarships were available from Caritas Nepal which sponsored kids who were past grade 10; the bus ride to the high school was an hour. I finished high school outside the refugee camp in Damak City at the Siddhartha private boarding school which was a higher secondary school. Then I was able to go to college at Biratnager College for a bachelor of science degree. I was not able to complete the degree at that time.

ELOPED

Elopement in Nepal was very common and widely used because of the limited finances and the social aspect of the caste system. Elopement is also common in Nepali communities in America due to the caste system. I met my husband, Mon, in the refugee camp and we regarded each other as friends/neighbors. We kind of grew up together socially, celebrating festivals and other events as kind of a community. Eventually we fell in love and eloped after dating 3 years in a hidden way starting in grade 10 for me and 11 for him. We continued to date in secret during college and eloped on June 24, 2004 on his birthday. When we married, we went to the biggest Hindu Temple in Nepal (Janakpurdham). We married in the evening with a few witnesses. We paid a priest 150 rupee which is equivalent to 1.20 American dollars for the marriage certificate. We didn't involve our family because we knew our families would not accept our union for social reasons.

My husband, Mon, was a boarding school teacher at that time and we went home to his apartment the next day from Janakpur. I started working with him in the boarding school teaching middle school kids. We planned to continue our education; however, I became pregnant after three months with our first child. This was quite an adjustment time for me because I grew up without a father and had no brothers. Living with a man was very unusual for me.

Mon in 1999
Bamboo bed, wall and ceiling.

*Mon putting a red dot on my forehead and the green
necklace which signify being married.*

Wedding photo taken the next day with sari.

UNEXPECTED PARENTHOOD 1

I became pregnant unexpectedly after 3 months of marriage. We were both very nervous and we were not well connected with our families at this time due to the strained nature of our relationships. We also had very little money. We got up enough courage to go to my husband's family to share the news during the Hindu festival, Dashain. After the celebration and sharing the news, we returned to our boarding school. I worked until I was 8 months pregnant and then returned to the refugee camp to deliver our baby. This was necessary because we were refugees and for our baby to be identified as a refugee, as well, we had to deliver there and verify her birth quickly in the camp.

Samikcha was born June 12, 2005, in the Amda Hospital in nearby Damak for a c-section after being referred there from the camp clinic. Otherwise I would have delivered in the hut where we lived. My husband was in the boarding school 5 hours away when I was in labor. He was unable to get to me because of civil unrest all around at that time. I was discharged from the hospital 3 days later to the hut in the refugee camp while Mon was still at the boarding school. When my daughter and I came home it was the rainy season. I stared out from inside the mosquito net and the bamboo sticks wall, frightened and alone.

On the 10th day the baby had a naming ceremony and the Hindu priest gave her the name Dambari, but we named her Samikcha. Thirteen days after her birth my husband came and finally saw his baby. He grabbed her and we cried to be united and held our baby together for the first time. Unfortunately, he had to return to the boarding school after a week to go back to work. I stayed there for a month to recover, and then returned to the apartment at the boarding school. I had an infected c-section wound and I had to walk on a muddy/slippery path to go to the bathroom, leaving my baby behind covered with a mosquito net. I was overwhelmed, lonely, febrile and in pain. I still tear up when I think about those days.

UNEXPECTED PARENTHOOD 2

When my first daughter was only 26 months old we moved to a different city called Sarlahi to work in the boarding school there. I became pregnant again unexpectedly. We both had a plan to work hard raising one baby for a few years. We didn't know the Lord at this time. He had other plans for our family. I gave birth again via c-section on April 19, 2008 to another beautiful daughter, Swakchha. Her sister was so sad that mom didn't bring home the brother she longed for that she said, "Take her back!" We didn't have any idea of the gender because of financial limitations so another girl it was. We previously had been in the process of coming to America and had planned to have our second child there, but because of health problems I was unable to travel. We waited for 11 months to move to America and lived at my mom's home until that time.

WAITING ON AMERICA WITH TWO BABIES

We went through a very, very thorough background check to vet us for citizenship in America. The process was over one year to complete to be able to come to America. Life was really hard as we had zero income and had to once again live in the refugee camp with a sparse food supply and poor living conditions with our two baby daughters. To cook food all refugees received charcoal. When the charcoal burns it pollutes the air terribly. Dust was everywhere and all surfaces were "muddy" with coal dust. Our girls were often sick with fever, ear infections and pneumonia.

We had no electricity or running water. We had to wait to get our water. We didn't have nutritious food for us or our daughters. In the winter the clothes would not dry; I was always washing their clothes because we had no diapers. I would hang the clothes outside to dry in the winter even though the sun didn't warm them enough to dry. In the summer it was super-hot under the plastic roof and we only had a hand fan to cool our babies.

We had no toys for the girls and no clean or safe area or space to put our girls down to play; we needed to always hold them. An old friend made us a makeshift cradle from an old sack and hung it off of the bamboo roof. During the night we would have heavy rains and storms and were afraid big branches from the trees would fall onto our house and hurt us. When the wind would start blowing, we would grab the babies and run to a house that didn't have trees overhanging their home. During the rainy nights the rain would seep into the house through the plastic roof. To protect our heads, we put plates or bowls on our heads to keep the water from dripping on us.

So many times, people were killed by cobras which are numerous in Nepal. We used a mosquito net because the mosquito population was thick. So many times, we didn't sleep because of storms and the anxiety we felt to wake up and hear bad news about someone being killed by falling branches or trampling elephants. Because this camp was at the edge of the jungle, elephants would come through looking for food and would trample people and break down the homes. They are considered gods in the Hindu religion and highly regarded so we could not hurt them in any way. Finally, the wait was over and we were cleared to move to the USA for the Third Country Resettlement through International Organization for Migration (IOM). We had survived with our babies for two years in that camp and a total of 18 years in the same refugee camp. On April 4, 2009, we left that refugee camp to come to America and a whole new world across the ocean.

These are water jugs that we would bring to the water tap which was turned on twice a day. We brought our jugs early as the line got very long later in the day.

Cooking food using firewood.

ON THE WAY TO AMERICA

We arrived in Kathmandu, Nepal, the capital city, on the same day that we left the refugee camp and stayed there for 3 nights before our flight with hundreds of other exiles. During these three days we underwent orientation about life in America and we, for the first time, received DIAPERS!! They gave us health checks once again and we all ate together and talked about where each family was headed and what we thought it would be like. We flew from Katmandu on April 7th to South Korea and spent the night there. This was our first international flight and we were very nervous and holding our babies so tightly. In the hotel in Korea I used a toothbrush and toothpaste, unaware that it would be charged to us and we had no money to pay for this so the kind Scout for our group kindly paid that bill for us.

We left Korea and flew into Chicago on April 8, 2009 with 4 dollars in our pocket and two babies. We had to leave the airplane due to some problems and we spent the night in a hotel room in Chicago. Our guide who received us in Chicago didn't explain to us everything about how to stay in a hotel. We all were very thirsty and there was a cup in the bathroom but we didn't use the glass because we never drank the water from the faucet that is close to a toilet in Nepal. The case worker brought a big chicken and some rice but no bottled water and we didn't know how to use the cups in the bathroom because we didn't understand that the water from the tap was ok for drinking. That whole night we went without water.

In the morning, my husband went out from the room, but he wasn't able to find water. He did find coffee which he called black water. We didn't like it much! Our case worker had instructed us to be ready by 10 am. We didn't understand that we could use the towels and washcloths, fearing we would be charged for them. We were afraid to even get the shower curtain wet, so we turned on the tap and took a kind of a spit bath and all shared one towel. I cleaned the room perfectly so that it was just as we had found it. We were so nervous and didn't know how to use the room well. I made the bed and cleaned the room to a spotless condition.

We used one dollar in Chicago to make a phone call to our families we knew from the refugee camp that had already arrived. We flew into Grand Forks, ND with three dollars to our name on April 9, 2009. A Lutheran Social Services caseworker and some volunteers from Faith Evangelical Free Church and Nancy Vrolyk were waiting at the airport to welcome us to North Dakota. There was a little snow on the ground which was new to our eyes. Then they brought us to our new apartment.

NO LONGER A REFUGEE

When we came to America we were given a home, food, job opportunities and more but the most valuable treasured thing we received was an identity. As refugees our citizenship, our homeland, our security, our rights and our protections were stripped from us. We were like orphans cast out into the world and needing to find a place to be. The USA gave us an identity with rights, privileges, security and protection. We were no longer defined as orphans or strangers. We were given a second opportunity to live life as humans with dignity and worth, with potential to achieve and the ability to rise up in the world. We didn't dare hope or dream for our future when we lived in the refugee camp...there was just no hope. We had no idea how to help our daughters or guide or lead them in such a hopeless dead-end lifestyle. But now these girls are living in the "land of opportunity" where they can be themselves, get an education, rise up and reach their fullest potential...where they matter because they are human. This new generation can teach others to be thankful and show an attitude of gratitude and be willing to invest, serve and protect this country that is not just a destination but is our home.

I was no longer a refugee.

OUR NEW LIFE IN AMERICA

We came to Grand Forks, North Dakota on April 9, 2009 and started living in an apartment 4 blocks away from Faith Evangelical Free Church. For the first month and a half we were busy getting established with orientation, baby care classes and other New American things. We received six months of food stamps and Medicaid medical insurance until we could find a job. We went for orientation at the job service office and applied for jobs in several places, anticipating calls for employment. At the same time, we went to the local community college to learn English and kept ourselves busy adapting to the good life here.

We used the bus to get from place to place. After two months, Mon got a job at the Super 8 in housekeeping. He made $7.24 per hour but with no fixed hours. We never knew how many hours he would be working. We both were so eager and anxious to find full time work with solid employment. I started working on the weekends and Mon worked during the week. I worked at the Road King Hotel in housekeeping. We were not making enough money to start saving with these jobs.

Both my husband Mon and I were afforded the opportunity to learn how to become interpreters and we took the test and passed the boards to become interpreters. We started working in the community at the hospital, dental offices and other places where interpretation was needed. We were so ambitious and anxious to improve and rise up. We were both interested in medical work so we attended CNA classes with help from Job Service who paid for those classes. We both attained CNA licenses. Mon finally got a call from Altru Hospital where he got a job working in Environmental Services, but I stayed home to care for the kids and did the interpreting job until our youngest could go to preschool. When she entered preschool, I applied also for a CNA job at the hospital. We both felt so proud that we were working in the medical field with a medical team of doctors and nurses. We both worked as CNAs and interpreters. We worked and worked and didn't really do much more. We just worked really hard for two and a half years. At that time, we became able to pay off our IOM loan that covered the cost to come to America. We were finally able to purchase a house in 2013 after leaving Bhutan in 1991.

INITIAL FRUSTRATING TIMES

We didn't have a car and we had lots of snow in Grand Forks. We used the city bus for transportation and had to spend a lot of time waiting outside in the wind and subzero temperatures to get to the clinic for the girls' shots and appointments. My husband, when learning to drive, mixed up the gas and the brake fluid and wrecked our cousin's car accidentally. It took us over a year to pay for the repairs. Lots of stressors.

We both struggled to get a job and ended up going to Northland Technical College for the CNA program and received CNA certificates. I applied for a CNA position at Altru Hospital. I had seen in a video at Job Services of a person in a business suit going for an interview for a job. I assumed that was what I needed to do, as well, and we both bought shoes and new suits to interview for a CNA job. However, they didn't hire me at that time because my English wasn't very good. I called Altru Human Resources and asked them to give me a try and see how well I could do. They hired me and then after a year they gave me the employee of the month award! I worked overnights and parented my girls during the day. I was so tired but thankful for this new opportunity. We are so thankful to Grand Forks Job Services because they taught us how to do an interview, create a resume and wear a fancy suit! We were both motivated to do better and never give up. We decided that Mon would attend school first, and then I would follow suit.

RAISING KIDS AS GODLESS PARENTS

We were raised in such extremely difficult circumstances under strong religious guidelines. It was acceptable to beat children if they stepped out of line. We could see right away that our methods of discipline were quite different from the American style of disciplining kids. We felt awkward and confused as to how to go about this in our own family. We went for parenting class but still failed with discipline several times.

SEEKING A CHURCH FOR SOCIAL ENRICHMENT

After waking up the first morning in our new apartment a welcoming, kind, smiling couple visited us, Linda and Gary Williamson. They offered to help us get settled and to see if we had any needs they could assist with. My kids ran right into their arms and we peppered them with questions regarding where to shop for baby supplies. Linda offered to help us until we felt comfortable navigating through the community to places that we needed to go. They invited us to their church if we would be interested in checking it out. I started going on Sunday mornings when I had the time to do so but my husband went every Sunday with the kids. We had a large Nepali community that also visited this church for the same reasons but none of us were seeking Christianity or Jesus at this time, including me. This church organized a Sunday school just for the Nepali, ordering Bibles in the Nepali language for us. Scott Korum and Michael Thieme were the leaders. Mon and I interpreted as best we could with our new English for the group.

Our girls were so happy in Sunday School. My husband really enjoyed the church and the Christians there but I only enjoyed the new friends and their warmth and kindness. This large group of Nepali in the Sunday school class existed for about two years. After one year attending this church, my husband said maybe we should stop worshipping all of our closet idols which I brought from Nepal. I was very scared at this prospect of possibly becoming a Christian and how it would affect our marriage and our families. I didn't want to suffer rejection or persecution. I grew up in a "people pleasing" culture and with the fear of man, and did my best to "perform" perfectly. I realized that becoming a Christian would be like breaking away from everything that I grew up with. I was not wanting him to bring this up again. I was very uncomfortable and scared.

I LIKED CHRISTIANS BUT NOT JESUS

I really liked Christians because they were so kind, helpful, encouraging, and supportive to me and my family. They taught us how to live in this new country. I didn't like Jesus or the thought of Him because I had enough of my own gods and goddesses and idols to worship already. If I were to accept Jesus, I would have to separate from everything I had previously believed and done for my gods. If I were to choose Jesus it would have dire consequences with my community and family over this choice. Rejection, isolation and possible persecution were real potential consequences of making this change.

I HAD MY PLANS BUT GOD HAS HIS

Isaiah 55:8-9, "For my thoughts are not your thoughts, neither are your ways my ways, declares the LORD. As the heavens are higher than the earth, so are my ways higher than your ways and my thoughts than your thoughts."

I never understood before the verses in Isaiah 55:8-9 that said, "God has higher plans than our own." He knows what is best for us as a good, perfect and Holy Father who cares so very much for His children. I had come to this church to better myself and get help rising up to a new identity and status, but God's intention was to draw my heart to His heart and give me a new identity through Christ, His perfect and holy, precious Son.

I had a growing curiosity.

When my husband mentioned a new life in Christ and that we were sinners who needed forgiveness and that because of Christ being perfect and holy He could pay for our sins and reconcile us to our Father God, I had a desire to know for understanding and knowledge only. I questioned my friend Linda, who would come and spend time with me, regarding my curiosity towards Christianity. I asked her to explain to me the facts and truths of the Christian walk. I thought when we debated, I would win her over to Hinduism because Christians have only one Triune God but Hindus have many, many gods. Every time I met with her I had questions prepared to prove to her that Christianity was false. It was a 'new' religion to me.

QUESTIONS AND ANSWERS WITH MY FRIEND LINDA

1. Isn't Christianity a "new" religion as it is not ancient?

Christianity is not a new religion. Jesus existed in heaven long before He was born, so He was from the beginning. John 1:1 says, "In the beginning was the Word (Jesus) and the Word was with God and the Word was God. He was in the beginning with God." John 1:14 continues that, "the Word became flesh and dwelt among us. We have seen His glory, the glory of the one and only Son, who came from the Father, full of grace and truth."

2. Isn't Christianity a western religion only?

Christianity is not a Western religion; rather Jesus was born, raised and died in Israel, which is in the Middle East. This is where the prophets prophesied about Him way before the development of western countries. After Christ returned to heaven, the church grew especially in what is now Turkey, Greece, and North Africa.

3. Can Christians intermarry with their family members?

No, Christians do not marry their own family members. There are accounts in the Bible where this sin was committed. This was not ordained by God, and did not turn out well.

4. How can we get salvation without karma?

Linda opened her Bible to the book of Ephesians 2:8-10 which says that we are saved by grace, through faith in Christ Jesus, not by our works. Grace is undeserved favor and a free gift from God.

5. Don't we have to have suffering to become good in God's eyes?

Because Christ suffered and died on the cross, He paid our penalty for sin and made relationship with God possible. It is through Him alone that we can be accepted and approved of by God; not by anything we can do. Isaiah 64:6 says that our good works of righteousness are like filthy rags before a perfect and Holy God. We don't have to suffer to save ourselves because Jesus paid the price with His suffering and if we believe in our hearts and confess with our mouths that Jesus Christ is Lord, we will be saved from our sins and transgressions.

6. How can I be a sinner if I haven't done anything really bad?

We are all sinners from birth not because of what we did, but because of our original parents, Adam and Eve, who brought sin to all mankind. Also, no one is righteous, not even one person. Sin includes not only the evil things which we have done but also choosing not to do good things that we have the opportunity to do. So even if we didn't do anything truly horrible, any sin is horrible to a holy and perfect God.

7. Isn't Christianity a cow-eating religion whereas Hindus worship cows and revere them as a god of wealth?

A cow is an animal created by God for us to use for food and for pulling plows. We are not defiled by eating them or other animals.

The Bible says in Matthew 15:11 that, "It is not what goes into the mouth that defiles a person, but what comes out of the mouth; this defiles a person."

8. Why isn't God married since my Hindu gods were married?

God's love is not of the romantic type, but rather for relationship with his creation and fellowship with them. Jesus didn't come to have human relationships with women in a romantic way. His concern was for reconciliation with God the Father between Him and His creation. His love is of a different nature, pure and holy.

9. Why did Jesus have to die?

Because God is holy and perfect, without sin, and unlike sinful humans, there had to be a way for sinful man to be reconciled to the God the Father. Jesus was fully human and also fully God. Because He lived a perfect life, He was pure and unstained by sin and could, therefore, sacrifice His blood for all who want to have a relationship with God the Father. He is the bridge between sinful humans and a perfect God. His blood washes us clean in God's eyes as the penalty was placed upon Jesus, rather than upon humans.

10. Why would a god sacrifice for me rather than me making the sacrifices to a god?

Any sacrifice a person could or would make to God could never be enough because He is perfect and holy and we are not. Jesus had to make the sacrifice in our place because He was perfect and His sacrifice was complete forever for the Christian. We love and serve Him out of love, but our works and love can never be enough to satisfy the need for a sin covering. God chose to sacrifice for us because He created us to be in a relationship with Him. But since we are not sinless and holy, we made this relationship impossible without someone--God--paying the penalty for sin on our behalf.

11. So are Jesus, God the Father and the Holy Spirit different?

God is a Triune God meaning that He exists as one but in three distinct persons; the Father, the Son, Jesus Christ and the Holy Spirit. They are equally God but distinct in their roles as God.

12. People said after someone becomes a Christian they will not suffer; is that right?

Eternally, we are one hundred percent free of suffering, pain and struggle. However, here on earth, when Jesus invites us into the Kingdom of God, it is not just for blessings and rewards, redemption and freedom all of which are beautiful in our human eyes, but we are, more importantly, invited into suffering. Suffering is not punishment for sins, or suffering for the sake of suffering but suffering that is a gift. This gift is a glory and an honor though, from a human standpoint, it is counterintuitive. However, this beautiful suffering is what deepens our faith, matures our hearts, souls and minds and gives us the greater ability to love God, be loved by Him and love others. This suffering is like pure gold and it is a high favor from God.

The Bible does not say anywhere that life is easy for Christians. Jesus said, "take up your cross and follow Me." The Bible gives the Apostle Paul's life as an example along with many others.

CONFUSION PERIOD

I continued to attend Sunday school, asking questions and listening to descriptions of Christ and Christlike living. I heard lots of terms that I didn't understand. I used this time to formulate an argument against Christianity and confirm my Hindu beliefs. My seeking was for knowledge only, never to convert to Christianity. I kept practicing my idol worship at home with the plastic bag of idols that I brought from Nepal. One day while interpreting in the Sunday school class, we happened to read Ephesians 2:8-9, "It is by grace that you have been saved through faith; it is not by works but a gift of God." After this class I struggled to understand the term "grace"; there is no concept of this in Hinduism. I knew only karma and practiced a lifestyle to serve the karma. Another Bible verse that troubled me and made me ponder is Matthew 20:28, "The son of man came to serve not to be served." So many terms like reconciliation, forgiveness, mercy and sanctification were all new and foreign to me. I didn't have a category in my heart or mind for these things of God. I started comparing Christianity with Hinduism to settle this spiritual quest for Truth, once and for all. These terms were stacked side by side in my mind for comparison. I spent many months contemplating and vetting these facts and truths.

SAVED BY GRACE VERSUS SAVED BY KARMA

"For it is by grace that you have been saved, through faith—and this is not from yourselves, it is the gift of God—not by works, so that no one can boast"
(Ephesians 2:8-9).

Hinduism has karma instead of grace. Karma is doing good things to ensure a good outcome depending only on one's abilities to perform.

Because I was raised in a strong Hindu family, I was told and taught to perform good karma. If we do good then we become good and if we do bad, we become bad. If we do good karma I could escape the 84 lakhs cycles of life. If I fail, I would have to live many lives as creatures other than human. But if I do, I will become a product of conception from a human and go right into another human existence. Along with doing good, if my funeral follows the procedures very well up to the standards, that would also allow me to avoid becoming a creature and go right into the next life cycle as a human. All of this depended upon me, my performance, and my ability to save myself.

If I strictly adhere to forbidden actions like avoiding untouchables and refraining from defiled foods such as pork, chicken and beef then I rise up in my striving for perfection, gaining points for myself for the future. In this way of life, we can't live and enjoy the moments and days we have because we are so busy trying to do just right and avoid wrong to ensure the future is good. We can't enjoy life as there is always something to be done to win points. No peace. Do this, do that, don't do this, don't do that without any reason or explanation...just suffering and sacrifice.

If I allow low caste people into my home or if I let them touch me, I become defiled which brings great shame and consequences accrued from disobedience.

Lots of food restrictions dictated the life of a Hindu person. We avoided this and that for this and that reason; never really understanding why or what this really accomplished. We didn't know why we were doing these things; we were just blindly following the traditions of our forefathers to show honor and be good.

RELIGIOUS SACRIFICE VS GOD'S SACRIFICE

I grew up witnessing the slaughter of innocent animals like goats, pigeons, and lambs every year for the appeasement of the god's requirement for a sin covering. We were instructed in families to guard and keep a specific animal chosen for the sacrifice in good condition for the presentation of a sacrifice. I had questions about sacrifices and the Bible. 1 Peter 1:19 states that Jesus Christ is the perfect and spotless Lamb of God that is without blemish or spot who laid down His life once for all humanity and became the ultimate sacrifice.

HINDU PRIEST VERSUS JESUS, THE ETERNAL HIGH PRIEST

I grew up worshipping the Hindu priests, and the men having to drink the water from washing the priest's feet to show deference to them. If a priest came to my house as a Hindu, I had to hire the priest's caste group to make his food so it would not be defied by a lower-caste person. I couldn't touch his food...he is supposed be there to serve me but he is actually the one being glorified and served. However, the Bible says that Jesus, our high priest, washed the filthy feet of his disciples, a lowly and meek Savior. He comes down to us to reach us and pull us up from the dirt to be reconciled to His perfect self.

Hebrews 4:14-16, "Therefore, since we have a great high priest who has ascended into heaven, Jesus the Son of God, let us hold firmly to the faith we profess. For we do not have a high priest who is unable to empathize with our weaknesses, but we have one who has been tempted in every way, just as we are—yet he did not sin. Let us then approach God's throne of grace with confidence, so that we may receive mercy and find grace to help us in our time of need."

John 13:14-17, "Now that I, your Lord and teacher, have washed your feet, you also should wash one another's feet. I have set you an example that you should do as I have done for you. Very truly I tell you, no servant is greater than his master, nor is a messenger greater than the one who sent him. Now that you know these things, you will be blessed if you do them."

TEMPLES AND PIGEONS

In my growing up years I was a witness to witchcraft and sorcery in the form of palm reading in which someone's future is predicted for blessing or a curse. In our family we practiced this to discern wisdom for hard circumstances or problems we needed answers for. I also witnessed animal sacrifice as payment for sin yearly with an offering of goats, sheep, pigeons, chickens and ducks. When my first baby, Samikcha, was 18 months old, she had a lot of trouble with food and eating. We took her to the hospital for testing and they said we needed to feed her more nutritious food because she was on the brink of malnourishment. We couldn't feed her even when we had good food for her; she just didn't want to eat. Some of our family suggested we try witchcraft to help with this situation. We invited the sorcerer and he came to our home and used pieces of rice and incantations. In the end he told us to go to the temple and sacrifice two pigeons and then take her to the river, which we worshipped, and bathe her in it. My husband wasn't interested in doing this but I had to listen to the elders and the witchdoctor to protect my daughter because of the darkness I was held in at that time.

Even though we took the pigeons to the priest, he didn't perform the ritual of blood shedding and sayings but rather took our pigeons and passed them right back to a marketeer to sell without performing anything that would have "helped" her at this time. He didn't release into the wild or sacrifice the pigeons, both of which would have been the proper thing in this ceremony for asking for healing and forgiveness of sin that we might have done wrong that would have caused this issue.

After this we worshipped the river with incense, flowers and fruits. We also had to make a disc with a hole in it out of cow dung and pour yogurt and water into it to worship it. We also made a plate out of banana leaf and in the middle, we made a candle out of ghee and a wool wick and lit this on the leaf and set it out to float in the river and watched it. The longer the candle floated, the more of the blessing we would receive. We also put money and flowers on the leaf boat and spoke some chants for worship and blessing. Some very poor boys would take those leaf boats and grab the money off of them because they needed the money so badly.

Nothing changed from all of this. She was 3 1/2 years old when we came to America and that whole time she still had the same eating issues. We tried so diligently to do our part in performing rituals and giving prayers and worship to help our child. This trip to the temple was the first significant religious rite that my husband and I had done together. Through all kinds of illness (even terminal illness), I have known that I have a high priest, Jesus Christ, who shed His blood for my sin and is able to heal all sickness if it is His will to do so. Nothing is impossible with God.

In Mark 10:27 Jesus looked at them and said, "With man this is impossible, but not with God; all things are possible with God."

I am so thankful to know that we are not able to change things by our own hands, will or rituals. It is only through the power of God, the mighty King of the world, that these types of matters can be changed. Through His mercy and grace and because of His sacrifice that paid for all sin once and for all we are free from such rituals and mystic thinking (Hebrews 9:28). So Christ was sacrificed once and for all to take away the sins of many and will appear a second time, not to bear sin but to bring salvation to those who are waiting for him. Hebrews 10:4 says that it is impossible for the blood of bulls and goats (and pigeons) to take away sins.

HINDU FESTIVAL OF LIGHT VERSUS THE LIGHT OF THE WORLD

I grew up celebrating the festival of light in Hinduism, regarding victory in war, family connection and love. It was beautiful to celebrate outside but there is was no spiritual gain or redemption available by participation. This festival involved worshipping cows, dogs, bulls and crows. A deep affection for family is expressed, especially to brothers and sisters. The cow was worshipped as the god of wealth and we also worshipped money and valuables. Though there was a lot of outward "beauty", real beauty was absent. These objects were not holy nor were they able to bless or help us in any way. Jesus is called the Light of the World (John 8:12) who comes down to earth to seek and to save the lost to offer forgiveness of sins and eternal salvation. His power is real and His promises are trustworthy. There is no darkness found in Him.

THE WAY, THE TRUTH AND THE LIFE

Buddha has said that he seeks peace and is searching for Nirvana. In Hinduism, no god can claim holy character or a desire to save, rescue or redeem. However, in the Bible Jesus says that He is the way, the truth and the life (John 14:6). Nothing can compare with Jesus. He is perfect, holy, loving, redemptive, full of grace and mercy, able to perform miracles and bring the dead back to life. He died but rose again, having victory over death. No grave can hold Him; no one can compare to Him.

In John 14:6 Jesus said, "I am the way and the truth and the life. No one comes to the Father except through me."

WORLDLY PEACE VERSUS THE PRINCE OF PEACE

The gods of Hinduism never provide peace without earthly war or gaining victory in the earthly world. Many of these gods seek peace via meditation or becoming solitary in life to find peace. But the Bible says that Jesus is the Prince of Peace who gives peace not as the world gives but, rather, peace that can alleviate fear and troubles in this life.

John 14:27, "Peace I leave with you; my peace I give to you. I do not give to you as the world gives. Do not let your hearts be troubled and do not be afraid."

Isaiah 9:6, "For unto us a child is born, unto us a Son is given. And the government shall be upon His shoulders and His name shall be called Wonderful Counselor, Mighty God, Everlasting Father, Prince of Peace."

"GODS" VERSUS THE BIBLE'S GOD

I grew up worshipping and serving uncountable gods and goddesses and creations such as the moon, the sun, plants, animals, snakes, elephants etc. These gods and goddesses bear the likeness of a human in actions. They sin just like humans and they establish families and participate in war like humans. There is no distinction of divinity; they are just like people. They exist for themselves offering nothing good but demanding glory and devotion and service with no return. They die and that is the end of them. But the God of the Bible longs for relationship and lowers Himself to the earth to serve, to take on the form of a man to understand and experience life as a human perfectly. Then He offers Himself to be a sacrifice to pay for the sins of the world. He seeks out humans to save and love them, not to make them unloved slaves.

John 1:14, "The Word became flesh and made His dwelling among us. We have seen His glory, the glory of the one and only Son, who came from the Father, full of grace and truth."

Matthew 20:28, "The Son of Man did not come to be served, but to serve, and to give His life as a ransom for many."

John 3:16, "For God so loved the world that He gave His one and only son, that whoever believes in Him shall not perish but have eternal life."

BREAD OF LIFE AND LIVING WATER

In the Bible, John 6:35 and John 7:37-39 state that Jesus is the bread of life and living water that never runs out. Assurance of flowing, unending sacrifice and offering are foreign in Hinduism. There is no guarantee or security as you can lose traction for your future by stepping out of line. Having your entire spiritual future on your own shoulders is a heavy burden that can't provide peace or security.

In John 6:35 Jesus declared, "I am the bread of life. Whoever comes to me will never go hungry, and whoever believes in me will never be thirsty."

In John 7:37-39, on the last and greatest day of the feast, Jesus stood and said in a loud voice, "Let anyone who is thirsty come to me and drink. Whoever believes in me, as the Scripture has said, rivers of living water will flow from within them. By this He meant the Spirit, whom those who believed in Him were later to receive. Up to that time the Spirit had not been given, since Jesus had not yet been glorified."

PURIFICATION

In the Hindu religion, before being able to participate in any rituals in the home, one has to be purified by drinking a sip of cow urine given by either a priest or an ordinary person. I strictly adhered to the ritual my whole life before participating in ceremonies. The Bible states that we can only be purified and made holy and acceptable to God by the covering and provision of Christ's offering of His perfect sacrifice. Because we are covered by His blood, we are free to worship God freely.

Psalm 51:2, "Wash away all my iniquity and cleanse me from sin."

Leviticus 16:30, "Because on this day atonement will be made for you, to cleanse you. Then, before the LORD, you will be clean from all your sins."

I John 1:9, "If we confess our sins, He is faithful and just and will forgive us our sins and purify us from all unrighteousness."

FORGIVENESS OF SIN

As a Hindu, when I did something wrong, forgiveness was not an option. The concept of forgiveness is absent from Hinduism; rather there is condemnation and isolation, punishment rather than discipline. If a high caste person marries a low caste person, the family of the high caste person will disown the married couple. They will be cut off from the family for a lifetime. The family can reject them forever and there is no forgiveness. Bitterness, anger, wrath, slander, malice is clung to and wielded rather than rejected for the sake of forgiveness and reconciliation. I witnessed this and was the victim of this treatment first hand. But God made a way for forgiveness by sending His perfect and holy son to atone for our sins and we stand in a constant state of being forgiven before Him because of Christ. God remembers none of our sins; He casts them into the sea and they are as far from us as the east is from the west.

Psalm 103:12, "Praise the Lord, my soul, and forget not all His benefits."

Isaiah 43:25, "I, even I, am He who blots out your transgressions for my own sake and remembers your sins no more."

Hebrews 9:22, "The law requires that nearly everything be cleaned with blood, and without the shedding of blood there is no forgiveness."

RELIGIOUS RANKING VERSUS CREATION IN GOD'S IMAGE

In Hinduism there is an automatic ranking of every human called a "caste system" in which a person has a certain value placed on them for no other reason than designating which level of approval they are born into. They are not judged or measured by who they are, what qualities they possess or any other measure. It only matters what they are born into.

There are four levels or castes in the Caste System. The first are highly valued and respected and do not associate in any way with the lowest caste member, called the untouchables. Genesis 1:27, Psalm 139 and Jeremiah 29:11 state that we are created in the image and likeness of God, knit together in our mother's womb, known by Him since the foundation of the world and created on purpose for His glory. God sees every person as infinitely valuable because each human is made in His image and worth dying for (Galatians 3:28). There are no rankings based on social status, wealth or education. Each person is equally valuable in God's eyes as we are all sinners in need of a Savior and all made in His likeness. God has no favorites and His goodness is offered freely to all humans. He offers special blessings through a relationship with Him for those who choose Him and are available for all humans if they so choose.

Galatians 3:28, "There is neither Jew nor Gentile, neither slave nor free, nor is there male and female, for you are all one in Christ Jesus."

FOOD DOESN'T DEFILE HUMANS

God says that all food is good for consumption and nutrition; we are not defied by eating anything. Matthew 15:11 says, "what goes into someone's mouth does not defile them, but what comes out of their mouth, that is what defiles them." Mark 7:19 says, "food doesn't go into their heart but into their stomach, and then out of the body. What comes out of the person's heart defiles them." The Bible says that all food is clean (Roman 14:20). Jesus ate with sinners most of the time when He was on the earth (Mark 2:13-17). But in my religion, most of the food was unclean for the upper caste group; if they even touch it, they get defiled. So many rules and boundaries about who can eat what and what you cannot.

ACCEPTANCE

In Hinduism, acceptance into a place of favor in the caste system is fragile and easy to lose. If your appearance is not favored (i.e. skin color), or you are born in the wrong family or are poor, there is no way to be accepted and included. You are always an outcast with conditional temporary acceptance and no assurance is available. Jesus welcomes anyone just the way they are. If we confess our sin, He is faithful and just to forgive us and keep no records of wrong.

I John 1:9, "If we confess our sins, He is faithful and just and will forgive us our sins and purify us from all unrighteousness."

Psalm 102:12, "As far as the east is from the west, so far has He removed our transgressions from us."

POWER AND VICTORY

In Hinduism, power and victory were to kill the enemies and celebrate it as a festival. All gods and goddesses died and they never rose again. Their story ended. There was no promise for salvation or redemption. But in the Bible, Jesus conquered death and rose from the dead on the 3rd day. He gave assurance of salvation by rising from the dead victoriously.

I Corinthians 15:4, That He was buried, that He was raised on the third day according to the Scriptures."

In Matthew 28:5-6 the angel said to the women, "Do not be afraid, for I know that you are looking for Jesus, who was crucified. He is not here; He has risen, just as He said. Come and see the place where He lay."

Luke 24:6-7, "He is not here; He has Risen! Remember how He told you, while he was still with you in Galilee. The Son of Man must be delivered over to the hands of sinners, be crucified and on the third day be raised again."

UNDENIABLE

I studied for almost 18 months in Adult Sunday school and had multiple conversations with my friend Linda. This has led me to a place of seeking more understanding about God, Jesus and Christianity. He doesn't keep records of wrong and I am saved by His grace. I am unconditionally accepted and loved. I felt for the first time in my life so relaxed and peaceful about my future and had something called hope. I had the choice to accept this or deny this but my heart was experiencing real changes and my mind was being transformed by the discoveries I was making. The Truth was undeniable.

ON THE FENCE

On the one hand, I was moved by beauty of the gospel, forgiveness of sins, eternal security, unconditional love and acceptance that I never had before. I had for the first time peace and hope and assurance. I would be free from guilt, shame, condemnation, insecurity, and the threat of a lost future. I had all of this beauty in my hands.

On the other hand, fear of rejection and isolation, condemnation and judgement, scorn and misunderstanding from the Hindu community and my own family lay as a likelihood that troubled me. Inside and outside the refugee camps I saw Christians being persecuted and mistreated. Was this worth the risk? Was it worth the loss? I saw the outcome of this decision; they were treated like they were dead and gone like a ghost from this world.

I SURRENDER ALL

My desire to counter the Truth faltered, my resistance faded and I independently decided to depend upon Jesus for my salvation and surrender to the Truth on my knees. I could no longer deny or resist the beauty and strength of the Truth of God's word and His character. There is no place in the universe that can compare to being the beloved in the palm of God's loving hand. Nothing can offer what only God can. I recognized Jesus as a perfect Savior and I confessed with my mouth that Jesus Christ is Lord and believed in my heart that God raised him from the dead. (Romans 10:9).

I am no longer confused about who I am. I am a child of God.

I AM SAVED!

I decided to move my life from the darkness and captivity to unconditional love and forgiveness, freedom, hope and joy through life in Christ Jesus. I am released from the fear of my future; I am safe in His mighty hand. I will never face rejection from Him. He will never deny me or my worth to Him. I don't have to kill myself striving in the cloak of uncertainty to try to win approval or gain goodness for a future. My future is assured, bought and paid for by the precious holy blood of Christ Jesus on the cross. No one can snatch me from His hand. He will never leave me or forsake me.

Deuteronomy 31:6, "Be strong and courageous. Do not be afraid or terrified because of them, for the Lord your God goes with you; He will never leave you nor forsake you."

In Hebrews 13:5 God has said, "Never will I leave you; never will I forsake you."

IDOLS FROM THE CLOSET

After I became a Christian, I packed up all the idols I had brought over with me from Nepal. I had them in the hallway like a shrine. The closet was decorated with colored paper to match the idols. I realized they are nothing. These "idols" that had threatened, pressured and held me in captivity my entire life no longer had any hold on me. I reflected on my actions towards these idols: feeding them, praying to them, washing and dusting them and worshipping them. I thought of all the incense I burned for them over my lifetime. I bagged them up and threw them in the trash can. As I was throwing away the physical idols from my closet, God was opening the eyes of my heart to see the idols in my spiritual closet. This began the process of getting rid of the idols in my heart.

"GODS" IN THE GARBAGE

Once I threw out the physical closet idols, the next morning, in the absence of these idols, I searched my heart for spiritual idols. Because my heart is the temple of the Holy Spirit, and God says for us to have no idols before Him (I Cor. 3:16, Exodus 20: 3-5), I didn't have much recognition at this time of idols in my heart. I was a young mom devoted to the care of my husband and girls and learning all about this new life in our new country and I was a baby Christian. As I grew and became more aware of what the Christian life entailed with regard to spiritual idols, I came to the realization that getting rid of idols in my heart would not be nearly as easy or quick as throwing out the others. It took me years to recognize how I made idols of my husband and children, money and work, status and chasing the American dream. Seeing the idols in my heart convicted me and started me on a journey of repentance and surrendering these unto the Lord.

SEEING THE CLOSET OF MY HEART WITH HIS LIGHT

What led me to start seeing these idols of my heart was a deep feeling of bitterness based on horizontal expectations. That is expecting things from people that only God can provide. I felt like I fell into a victimized frame of mind because I was a cancer survivor and new Christian who had forsaken the security of self-reliance, worshipping the old gods. Now I wanted the replacements of security, love, affirmation and acceptance of all things that life in Christ offers, but I was seeking them from people rather than from the source from which they all come. I knew I needed to have my expectations from God, a vertical surrender, but my heart desired human fulfillment more. I longed to be verbally affirmed and praised for all the hard work I did of loving and pouring into people. I wanted a person to tell me I was a good mom and wife; I was desiring people to give me worth and identity through their praise and acknowledgement. My heart was weary and led me to seek more than just people for what I really needed. I eventually realized that expectations have to be vertical for a believer, to look to Him for everything. He is the God that supplies all of our needs according to His riches in glory in Christ Jesus. My idols of expectations, bitterness, self-dependence…I decided to live my life throwing these away day by day, moment by moment.

Philippians 4:19, "And my God will meet all your needs according to the riches of His glory in Christ Jesus."

I Corinthians 10:31, "So whether you eat or drink or whatever you do, do it all for the glory of God."

Colossians 3:17, "And whatever you do, whether in word or deed, do it all in the name of the Lord Jesus, giving thanks to God the Father through Him."

FAITH OVER FEAR

After I became a Christian, even though I knew how good God was and how safe I am in His gentle care, I still, like all believers, struggled with my flesh and with fears and bitterness. Fear had a big grip on me when I was very sick with cancer. And when I went through some personal struggles I deeply feared about my future and my security. I knew in my head what the Truth was, but I had to walk with Him moment by moment sometimes. It was the battle of the flesh and I needed to allow the Holy Spirit to transform my mind and help me in my unbelief. God is SO much bigger than our fear and our struggles. He has shown Himself to me time and time again; I would cry out to Him and call to Him for help. All of God's children can call on Him in times of trouble and He will always help them.

Philippians 4:13, "I can do all things through Him who gives me strength."

Hebrews 11:6, "Without faith it is impossible to please God, because anyone who comes to Him must believe that He exists and that He rewards those who earnestly seek Him."

WHY DO I NEED GOD?

The most critical reason that any human needs God is because we are sinners, born under the curse of sin. Every person is made in God's image, as His own creation. Everything is made by Him, for Him and through Him, but people are special. People are the only created things are made in the very image of God Himself. He created people for the primary purpose of having a relationship with Him. He wants a relationship with every human. He created us to love Him and because of His goodness and perfection to worship and obey Him. He offers us protection, security, hope, peace and goodness because He is perfect and holy. It is because of who He is that any person can have hope. Money, status, gold, beauty and importance will never truly satisfy. It will for a little while but our hearts are created for things not of this world...we long for more because we are made for more. It is only through a relationship with Jesus Christ, God the Father and the Holy Spirit that all of our deepest needs and longings can be met.

We humans long for love, acceptance, meaning in life, purpose, security, to be cherished and unconditionally accepted and approved of. No person is capable of this type of love, because every person is a sinner. We are, because of the God that lives in us when we are saved, called to love others unconditionally as well; we are called to be like Jesus and through dependence on and surrender to Him, we can in some measure, accomplish this. This is for sure and for certain though no human can give us what we really want and need. God is perfect, loving, kind, holy, righteous, mighty, omniscient, omnipresent, eternal and to the very core GOOD. He is everything and all we need.

All people are sinners in the world because of Adam, and all people need forgiveness. We need God's grace. From one man's disobedience, death came to all people. But through one person's obedience, we are saved. We are not saved by our karma God alone can save us

Romans 5:12, "Therefore, just as sin entered the world through one man, and death through sin, and in this way death came to all people, because all have sinned."

Ephesians 2:8-10, "For it is by grace you have been saved, through faith—and this is not from yourselves, it is the gift of God— not by works, so that no one can boast. For we are God's handiwork, created in Christ Jesus to do good works, which God prepared in advance for us to do."

Praise the Lord!

A NEW CREATION IN CHRIST

2 Corinthians 5:17 says that if anyone is in Christ, he is a new creation. The old has passed away; behold, the new has come!

As I contemplated the whole concept of being a new creation in Christ, I took all of this beautiful truth in deeply and carefully considered how I was going to live my life from here forward as such. I was working full time at the hospital to make our life beautiful in America and growing in Christ. The first thing I thought about as a new creation was leaving behind the bondage of manmade religions and rules and was so free from the slavery and fear of rejection. Being a new creation doesn't mean we will live a problem free in life here on earth. Being a new creation is having a new identity through Christ Jesus. It means having the blessings and privileges of being a child of the one true God. Yes, we walk through the valleys and we walk on the mountain tops...through it all God is with us, in us and working through us always.

I John 3:1, "See what great love the Father has lavished on us, that we should be called children of God! And that is what we are! The reason the world does not know us is that it did not know Him."

John 1:12, "Yet to all who did receive Him, to those who believed in His name, He gave the right to become children of God."

SHATTERED DREAMS

I started feeling weak and was losing weight. I was so busy working hard and taking care of my kids at home that I didn't address it. I finally went to my primary doctor on March 6, 2014 and then to ER on the 7th with my friend Linda as I was feeling so sick. I went back to my primary doctor, who didn't find anything wrong. She prescribed pain medicine and sent me home.

On Sunday, March 9, I wasn't able to go to church or work. After church my doctor friend, Marsha Lange, visited me because she knew I wasn't feeling well. She saw quickly that I wasn't well and admitted me to the hospital for testing. It was discovered that my hemoglobin was very low, platelets were low and the rest of the lab work abnormal. All night they transfused me, and the next day I was transferred to the Roger Maris Cancer Center in Fargo, North Dakota. I was so sick that I didn't remember much about that night or the trip to Fargo.

When I woke up at 9 a.m. I saw doctors, nurses and my family around me. I wasn't sure where I was or why I was there and they informed me that I had blood cancer and that I needed a bone marrow biopsy that day to determine what type of cancer I had. I could not believe that after all I had lived through that I would get a diagnosis like this; it was devastating. My life was so happy and good. I was young, healthy, I exercised and ate healthy foods. It felt like all my dreams were shattered. My daughters were 8 and 5 years old; they didn't really understand what was going on. I had so many dreams of a big, beautiful life in America with my husband and my girls. I was shocked and scared but I trusted God and remembered a lot of scriptures during that time that comforted me: Psalm 23, Psalm 56:3, Isaiah 41:10, 2 Corinthians 4:16-18 and more. These brought me great comfort, security and stability during this unknown and scary journey.

Psalm 23:1-6, "The Lord is my shepherd, I shall not be in want. He makes me lie down in green pastures, He leads me beside quiet waters, He restores my soul. He guides me in paths of righteousness for His name's sake. Even though I walk through the valley of the shadow of death, I will fear no evil, for you are with me; your rod and your staff, they comfort me. You prepare a table before me in the presence of my enemies. You anoint my head with oil, my cup overflows. Surely goodness and love will follow me all the days of my life, and I will dwell in the house of the Lord forever."

Psalm 56:3, "When I am afraid, I put my trust in you."

In Isaiah 41:10 God says, "Do not fear for I am with you; do not be dismayed for I am your God. I will strengthen you and help you; I will uphold you with my righteous right hand."

2 Corinthians 4:16-18, "Therefore we do not lose heart. Though outwardly we are wasting away, yet inwardly we are being renewed day by day. For our light and momentary troubles are achieving for us an eternal glory that far outweighs them all. So we fix our eyes not on what is seen, but on what is unseen, since what is seen is temporary, but what is unseen is eternal."

MISUNDERSTANDING THE GOSPEL

When I was suffering with my cancer, I had so many different friends from different denominations ask me why I could get cancer if I was a Christian. They accused me of not doing something right or not doing something else well enough and that is why I got cancer. This didn't sway me in the least. It was an opportunity for me to share with them my confidence in God's word that states that we live in a fallen world, full of pain and sorrow but that this earth is not our home. We are temporary visitors here but our eternal home is in Heaven with God.

I showed them in the Bible many people who had suffered including our Savior...who is called the suffering Savior. Abraham, Moses, Noah, David, Joseph, the prophets, all the apostles and our own Jesus suffered on this earth during their lives. Suffering has consequences but much suffering is just part of life on this planet. Romans 8:17 says that, "we are invited into suffering with Christ so that we may also share in His glory." Philippians 1:29 states that, "it has been granted to believers on behalf of Christ to not only believe in Him but also to suffer for Him." Romans 8:20 says that, "all creation is subjected to frustration not by its own choice but by the will of the one who subjected it, in hope that the creation itself will be liberated from its bondage to decay and brought into the freedom and glory of the children of God."

GRIEF WHILE HOLDING ON BY A THREAD

I was so very sick from the chemotherapy and not doing well at all. I received chemo from March to June, staying in the hospital most of that time. Because of my frailty, I had life-threatening fungal and bacterial infections. I had severe colitis, needed daily blood infusions, and had a super low white blood cell count. The oncologist decided to transfer me to the Intensive Care Unit (ICU). My white blood cell count dropped even further there to below 0.5, with normal being 4.5-11. The doctor said I would not live if my blood count didn't go up within a few days.

Our family started grief counseling with our daughters to help them understand what death is. My family and relatives from all over the U.S. along with many friends came to see me in Fargo to say goodbye even though I was in neutropenic isolation. I wanted to say goodbye to my friends.

LAST CHANCES

When I was told I wasn't going to survive, the first thoughts were for my daughters. I was concerned about how my husband was going to raise them and how their walk with the Lord was going to happen. I held each of their hands in mine and told them and talked to them about living with Jesus here on earth so they could come to Heaven some day and be reunited with me there. I asked them to sing "I have decided to follow Jesus" to me and other Sunday School songs. All I could focus on was my girls. Moms worry, even when they are dying, about their kids.

Our oldest daughter was trying to grasp the meaning of death and separation. She cried a lot during that time as did I. The youngest with her spunky nature and problem-solving mind told me to be sure to take my cellphone to Heaven with me so I could face time her when I got there. Oh, the thoughts of a child. It broke my heart into a million pieces. I never questioned

God's choice for my life and my daughters' lives; He is so good and trustworthy. I knew and was comforted by the fact that I was not in control. I would ask my Christian friend, Rachel, to read scripture to me such as 1Corinthians 15:52, "In the twinkling of an eye I will wake up with Jesus" and also singing spiritual songs to me.

I still didn't want to leave my babies but I trusted Him through it. I so longed to see them grow up, achieve and excel in this beautiful country and see them marry and have their own families and walk with the Lord their whole lives. This was all I truly longed for. I would braid their hair and my heart would ache wondering who would do this for them in the future. All my thoughts were on my girls and their life without me. I thought about all the nights I went into their rooms and would sing scripture songs, especially Psalm 23 and John 8:12, and do devotions with them until they fell asleep. I talked with them about their futures and what they wanted to be when they grew up. I spoke to them about following Jesus with their whole hearts their whole lives. I prayed over them while holding their hands for God to protect them and keep them close through deep tears. I exhorted them to be kind and loving to each other and treat each other well.

I was comforted that they were being raised in this beautiful country with freedom and human rights where they would be safe, protected and well cared for. I was thankful my husband was with them even in my absence. We also had good friends, the Snyders, that brought the girls to Fargo to visit me once or twice a week and then they also stayed at their house. The girls also stayed with my mom and sister when I was in the hospital. I was also comforted by my Christian friends, Amy, Shawn, Ginnie and Kelli, who came to visit me frequently and was so thankful for them. Also, my friend Linda called me every morning and read Scripture which gave me great peace.

When I think on it more, I remember the scriptures about worry and fret and that God is already in tomorrow and that we are not to worry because of Him and His goodness (Matthew 6:34). This brought me great comfort in my struggle to rest in Him peacefully and trust Him for the future.

But I also boldly asked for a miracle healing for my body.

THE GOD OF MIRACLES

In the sorrow and saying goodbye to friends and family, my cousin Bhima who lives in Fargo helped so much to bring my kids to the ICU and would stay until midnight and took care of them a lot for me. My mom and sister came to say goodbye to me and my sister Tika wept and wailed in sorrow. My youngest sister couldn't come but she facetimed me and she was very, very sad and crying so very hard. She was due to give birth and could not be there. They were so upset, hopeless and sad and my friend Rachel drove them home to Grand Forks after 1 a.m. My good friend Ginnie and her husband stayed with my husband Mon and I overnight to be present until I entered eternity. I had a nurse constantly with me, I was never alone. I had to do my living will directives about how to die and what measures I would take; I decided on intubation only.

However, on the morning of the 5th day, they drew blood for labs and something incredible happened. My white blood count was going up a bit. The doctor said this was a very good sign. Ginnie called everyone and said my count was up a bit ...God was making a way when there was no way. Within a few days my WBC returned to normal. I was able to be moved to a regular room instead of the ICU.

My daughters visited me in my hospital room after being transferred from the ICU at Sanford Hospital in Fargo.

When I got moved to the normal floor my girls were so joyful that they jumped onto my bed and rode with me to the room. We were all overjoyed and astonished and thankful! Bhima came and just cried tears of joy for this good news. My cousins from different states, uncles, aunts, my husband's family came to visit me because I was out of ICU. My husband and I were asking what the plan was from here. The doctor said, "If I were you, I would stop aggressive chemotherapy and wait until your strength comes back and then go to maintenance chemo." My quality of life greatly improved and I was happy to be home to recover from the aggressive chemo.

I was discharged from the hospital and came home and established with another oncologist in our town for the maintenance chemo. When I started this in Grand Forks, I again had to be hospitalized and had a biliary bag placed because of gall bladder pain and inflammation. I could not have surgery because my white blood cell count dropped again and my lungs had filled with fluid bilaterally. They put in a chest tube on both sides to drain the fluid from my lungs and I stayed hospitalized for another 27 days. After I recovered from all of this acute infection they removed my gall bladder and I was finally able to be discharged home again!

FREE AT LAST!

I was so, so weary and was really excited about increasing my quality of life after all of this drama and hardship. I wanted to live my life again!! We asked my oncologist to pause the chemo for one month so I could just be human again and enjoy my life and my family and make memories with them. My husband was in nursing school during all of this time. Some friends wanted to help our family get away and supported us to go to Florida for a vacation. Because I was so weak and wobbly and our kids were still small, my husband couldn't manage all three of us. So, my dear friend Amy came with us to help as did my niece, Nisha. I had the opportunity to have wheelchair assistance but thanks to my Heavenly Father I didn't have to use it.

I went on all the scary rides with my girls because compared to what I have been through, this was really doable. It gave me a new perspective at that time because before this time I was too afraid to do these types of rides and am still today, but that was my moment to live big and enjoy my time there and the girls to the fullest.

I was strengthened more and more each day, even more than I had prayed for. I asked for a week to really enjoy and partake of this time but He was so good and generous to me to give me even more.

In 2015 I started visiting my cousins and family in different states. I took this opportunity to share the Gospel of Jesus Christ with them because of what He did in my life and how He showed His goodness to me through this terrible trial. I was able to see my girls develop in the sports like gymnastics, cheer, soccer and volleyball. I was so overcome with thankfulness that I was alive and able to watch my girls learn and thrive I shed many tears of joy and thankfulness every time I watched them. In 2016 I decided to work some at Spectra Health as an interpreter as the need arose. I had bone marrow biopsies done every six months and at every visit the results were good.

I was cancer free!

Memories from Disneyworld, 2014

NEW BELIEVER STRUGGLES

As a new believer I became aware of some things I needed to address in my own heart. I grew up in Hinduism without any concept of forgiveness or unconditional forgiveness. I had a giant wad of unforgiveness stuck in my heart, weighing me down. I wasn't able to give it over to the cross in its entirety, but just bit by bit. This was a struggle and impacted my spiritual health. I realized this and sought out Godly counsel from friends and went for some Christian counseling, too. I read books based on their recommendations.

My understanding of forgiveness was that it was two ways. That if I forgave someone, they would also then forgive me. Before I learned to forgive I had a lot of bitterness. Bitterness is like an arrowhead that goes in smoothly but when it has to be removed it rips and causes pain. Even though I knew the verse in 1 Peter 5:7 that says, "cast your burdens upon the Lord and He will care for you", I still struggled to cast them off and not hold onto them.

It felt good to hold onto bitterness in a way because it made me feel like I had some power to wield if I needed it. It, however, is a poison and instead of poisoning the person we are bitter at, it actually poisons the one who holds onto it. It is like drinking poison and expecting the other person to die.

Some people encouraged me to just let these things go in a way that I am not processing the pain but just forgetting in the name of Christianity. However, you can't forgive something you are not willing to feel or think about. You have to feel to heal. We shouldn't have to pretend to forget. Anything we refuse to feel, deal with, and heal from, sits in the darkness, grows more powerful and 'deals' with us instead. We are not in control; it, instead, has control over us. I have learned that sometimes I will forgive but will not be forgiven. I had to learn about boundaries and unconditional love. I can do my part and then remain soft and willing toward another even if they do not respond in a positive way or offer forgiveness in return, like Jesus forgave us on the cross, when we were ignorant and in the darkness. From this example I learned about unilateral and bilateral forgiveness. The Bible tells us to forgive "70 times 7" or, in other words, keep forgiving as long as it is needed.

Ephesians 4:32, "Be kind and compassionate to one another, forgiving each other, just as in Christ God forgave you."

Romans 5:8, "But God demonstrates His own love for us in this: While we were still sinners, Christ died for us."

In Matthew 18:21-22 Peter came to Jesus and asked, "Lord, how many times shall I forgive my brother or sister who sins against me? Up to seven times?" Jesus answered, "I tell you, not seven times, but seventy times seven."

BACK TO NEPAL IN DECEMBER, 2017

I was able to make a trip to Nepal with my friend Amy in December of 2017 to see the orphanage centers and visited women who had been rescued from human trafficking (Beauty for Ashes). We were able to see the beautiful mountains and visit with friends. We also had many opportunities to care for, show compassion to and love on people in dire circumstances with great needs. Because of Jesus in my heart, I was moved to help them in any way I could like giving them food, socks for the shaking and cold, dirty feet, and hot tea for the cold and trembling hands. I was able to hug widows, wipe their tears and comfort them and share about Jesus with them so they could understand for the first time what a real and living hope is. All of these offerings were for His service because of God's love for me, He gave me love for others who are hopeless. In the orphanages we listened to the hard and sad stories of how the children ended up in an orphanage. I was able to share my testimony in church.

Because of some political troubles we were, unfortunately, unable to visit the refugee camp. But God provided money from someone to use for ministry and we were able to give money to a 6-year-old boy who had cancer for his chemotherapy and surgery. This family heard we were coming to Nepal and they wanted to come and visit us. His family drove for 8 hours to come and see us. I was so humbled and moved to tears to be able to hold him in my arms. I cried and rejoiced at the same time. We celebrated his birthday together that day. This was the most joyful moment during our trip.

We had a wonderful family that hosted us while we were in Nepal. My husband and I had rented a home from them when we were outside the refugee camp working at the boarding school. They didn't want us to stay in a motel and wanted to host us in their home. We really enjoyed all of the small blessings of fellowship and fun on this trip. We also enjoyed visiting a Nepali missionary family and drove 6 hours to visit another orphanage.

I felt so satisfied and happy to share the Gospel with everyone we met and refreshed by the fun and blessing of it all.

A Nepali missionary family, the Lamas, we visited in Nepal.

The village is similar to my childhood village in Bhutan.

Remembering my childhood and the basket I carried for firewood or water.

The Himalayan Mountains in Nepal

THE CZECH REPUBLIC IN 2019 AND ISRAEL IN 2022

I was given an opportunity through Faith Evangelical Free Church to go to the Czech Republic on a mission trip. I had so many conversations with people that were at the camp where the Bible lessons were held. They wondered why I became a Christian as Hinduism is such a beautiful religion. That opened the door to many significant conversations about Jesus.

I had a desire to go to Israel and walk where Jesus walked and was happy to go there with a group. I was amazed seeing all the historical places which clearly speak to us about the reality of Jesus and the Gospel message!

The City of David, Jerusalem, behind me.

Mount of Olives in Israel, 2022

LOOKING BACK WITH OPEN EYES

As I reflect on my struggles before I was a believer, I especially remember the trauma of not having a place to give birth to my second child. I felt deep sorrow. I also struggled with trying to win people's hearts with all my energy, but I failed. I wanted unconditional love and care in my time of need. I was desperate for security. I didn't get it. Even though I wasn't a Christian, I could see that all people loved conditionally based on their moods and my behaviors.

My history of being an outsider, of sorts, started because my dad passed away and my mom had circumstances that required me to live with a cousin and then with an uncle for a while. I longed to call for my dad and mom like my cousins did; I longed to feel a part of a family. I wanted to feel like I really belonged. I wanted to be a daughter, cherished and loved by my parents. I was living like an orphan because of hard circumstances. Even though I was loved and cared for so well by other family members, it still hurt to not be tucked in securely with my own family.

All of the weight of this came surging back up to my heart during this hard time when Samikcha was 2 and I was expecting our second baby and just didn't have a place to settle in after having our baby like other people did. This insecurity magnified my hurt from my childhood. I felt unloved, rejected, unaccepted, ugly, like an obligation or a burden even though I was welcomed by my uncle and aunt who loved me like their own. My grandpa and grandma loved me too, though I didn't get to see them that often. I would lie in my bed at night when everyone went to sleep and wish and long for my family to be together. I cried a lot during those times of loneliness.

Living at my cousin Maya's home for a year before I lived at my uncle's house, I have so many good memories. They loved me but I wanted my dad and missed my mom and sister. I can't imagine how I could leave them.

I see it now with different eyes. I see that if I had all my longings met and felt secure and satisfied in this earthly life, I would not have a desire or need for a Heavenly Father who offers unconditional love. I now realize that what I was longing for was not available from humans. Only a perfect, loving Heavenly Father was able to give me everything my heart really deeply desired. His love and acceptance are nothing I can earn and nothing I can lose. I didn't have to win His approval or convince Him I was worth loving. He loved me from before the foundations of the earth were set with an everlasting love. When I was rejected and despised in so many areas of my life I never thought in my understanding that I could have peace, security, hope, comfort and unconditional love ever in my life.

But I have everything I really want, resting in His goodness and might, His deep character as a perfect Daddy and protector and provider. I can crawl into His lap anytime I want and I am deeply loved and wanted by Him, so much so that He gave his only precious Son to die for me. He will never leave me, I always have a home with Him, He is my rock, my salvation and my shelter (Psalm 62:6-7).

FATHER'S FOUNDATION

Because my father died when I was only 6 months old, I do not have any memories of him. I would dream of what life would be like if my father was still alive and my mom, my sister and I were an intact family with him. My foundation of my father's home in Bhutan stood, surrounded by many different types of fruit trees. I would walk down from my uncle's home and stand on that foundation and dream about what life was like before he died. How my life would be so different had he still been alive. I would imagine our family would be beautiful and our life good because we were together. I imagined myself climbing on his back and being carried around like a treasure. I would sit and listen to the birds and eat and eat so much fruit. Watching my uncle and his family love each other, care for each other and cherish each other tweaked pain and envy in my own heart. My uncle tried to replace my father and give me a strong, beautiful, loving and connected family but it was not the same; I really wanted this with my own parents.

My mouth longed to speak the word "daddy". I would contemplate these things deeply as a small girl and my heart ached with these thoughts. We are created with a longing for family connection, security, belonging, which forms our internal foundation that is built upon all our lives. My foundation had cracks and holes, missing pieces because of the loss. The loss and lack of his love and care contributed to my worth and identity and I was fragile and unsteady. My little girl heart knew things were not as they should be. I deeply felt the void of a father and traditional family life. As I stood upon that broken, rocky foundation that my father built with his own hands, I was left to dream about what could have been; I grieved.

This is an empty foundation similar to one that my father had built and still remains.

The loss of an earthly father made the gift of a Heavenly father so much richer to me when I was saved in 2012. The earthly foundation that I was so convinced would satisfy and bring me a feeling of completion, was actually the foundation of Christ Jesus who is the cornerstone, the most valuable and essential stone of any solid foundation. It was also the only one that could truly complete me and gives me what every human longs for and that is a relationship with Him through His Son, Christ Jesus. Psalm 68:5 says, "God is the father to the fatherless; I am no longer unidentified, orphaned, displaced or unknown." He knit me together in my mother's womb and knew me before the foundation of the earth (Psalm 139:13). The joy that filled my heart and quieted the sorrow of the loss of my earthly dad elated me. I felt for the first time like a princess, cherished and highly valued because I found my lost identity in Him. He calls me precious, beautiful, intentionally created, princess, daughter of the Highest, redeemed, beloved and worth dying for. Anyone who has a warped sense of identity and worth due to loss of a father, trauma or abuse can come to Jesus who is the cornerstone that can't be destroyed or lost and is the gate to our Heavenly Father.

The Scripture says that Jesus is the cornerstone, the most important stone in the foundation of a home (Matthew 21:42, Psalm 118:22). Jesus took on flesh and dwelt among us humans where He was seen and touched. He became the actual cornerstone in every way (Ephesians 2: 19-22, Isaiah 28:16). Most Nepali people from Bhutan had to leave the country and left their foundations behind. If we have the most expensive, valuable foundation on the earth, it will eventually be destroyed and fade away. Even if we gain the whole world, we will lose our lives (Matthew 16:26).

However, the foundation I am now standing on is one that can't be lost, taken or destroyed. We long so naturally and deeply for our earthly, imperfect fathers. Because we are made in God's image for a relationship with Him, we long for Him ever more, even if we are unaware of it because it is built into our hearts as each of us are His precious creation. Because we see through a broken filter as humans, our longings and desires seem so compelling and critical. We simply are unable to realize our value until our view is perfected through a relationship with Christ. It is only in relationship with Him that our identity and worth becomes known.

PROMISED LAND

God rescued the Israelites from captivity in Egypt and led them through the desert to the promised land of Canaan, the land flowing with milk and honey (Exodus 3:8). They had to travel 40 years through the wilderness to finally arrive (Joshua 5:6). To take possession of the promised land the Israelites had to fight the enemies of God to win it.

When we were rescued from the wilderness of the refugee camp we were so blessed to come to the land of milk and honey but we didn't have to fight for it. It took only 18 hours for us after 18 years in the "desert." Just like God provided food for the Israelites in the desert, He provided for us in the refugee camp. We never knew that God had planned for us to be refugees much less to be sent to live in America! We were free to enter into this beautiful land.

God always has a purpose for allowing us to be captives, but He always is ready to rescue us and set us free, for it was for Freedom that Christ died. I really didn't understand His mighty power, even though he had rescued me from the refugee camp until I read this account in the Bible. God promised the Israelites that they could go to a land flowing with milk and honey. I am thankful God brought us to this country where we can always have the milk and honey if we work and eat pomegranates we don't have to plant!

My promised land is America, the land of opportunity and freedom. I will never disrespect or take advantage of this country and I pray for this country and for God's will to be done here. My eternal promised land is Heaven which is also something I could never earn, but another free gift with unending blessings.

I WILL NEVER TAKE FOR GRANTED

I will never take this American life blessing for granted. I am in this country not because I deserve to be but because of God's mercy and grace to me and to my family. Running water, hot water, electricity, washing machines, cars, job opportunities and more were just unknown in my homeland. In Bhutan, water was a difficult thing to get. We had to walk a mile one way to gather water. We took a bath with cold water in the summer and we had to warm it up in the colder weather and carry it to a makeshift bathroom with plastic walls. We were blessed. Some people in Nepal and India in worse circumstances drink filthy water from the river. To be able to walk to a clean sink, turn a handle and have fresh, clean water -whether warm or cold- come out is like a miracle and I will never take it for granted.

If we are honest, hard workers, we are able to make a good life with enough clothes, shoes, and food. We never had shoes to wear in the winter and in the summer, we used banana leaves to make shoes in the refugee camp. Even something as simple as an umbrella is a luxury; we had to use banana and elephant ear leaves as we ran through the rain to our classrooms.

Growing up, we never had a mattress of any type; we had to use very uncomfortable bamboo with a very thin blanket. Oh, the wonder of mattresses and blankets, sheets, pillows and even heated blankets here in America. Even the poorest person in America has a blanket and pillow and some type of bed to sleep on. Food in America is abundant and in great variety found absolutely everywhere. In the refugee camp we never had good quality food or enough to eat. Even to brush our teeth is a privilege. Many Nepalis had such bad teeth that they were unable to be fixed because they never had toothbrushes and toothpaste. There was no dollar store in Nepal, either.

APPRECIATE BUT NEVER TAKE ADVANTAGE

Anyone who lives in America, whether they were born here or allowed to move here, is highly favored and blessed. The American people have so generously welcomed international friends and shared the abundance of goodness in America with them. This should never be taken for granted or taken advantage of. No one deserves to live here...it is a mercy and a blessing. No one should ever lie or cheat the government or hate its citizens and disrespect them. People who cheat must have forgotten the dire circumstances from which they were rescued and many foster a poor attitude of ingratitude in disrespecting this country and its citizens; this should not be who we are.

HOSPITAL BEDSIDE CITIZENSHIP

I became a citizen of a country for the first time in the hospital when I was expected to die. I was very sick and my good neighbor who regularly checked on my condition with my husband, when he heard I was in critical condition, made connections with the citizenship office. He notified them of my dire situation and immediately the next morning they came to my hospital bed and issued the citizenship oath to both my husband and me. I was very fragile, unable to raise my hand to make my oath, I was weak and trembling but I was given citizenship and a U.S. flag was put on the wall in my room.

This was in August of 2014 when I gained earthy citizenship in this great country. I had applied for citizenship before I became sick. When I was in the hospital they called me for the interview at the office and the Doctor discharged me for a bit for this specific purpose.

I passed the first interview even though I wasn't able to read the book but I had listened to it read on audio. The nurses who were hearing this playing in my room commented that they, too, were learning alongside me about the U.S.

We knew our girls would be automatic citizens if my husband and I became citizens and I really wanted to do this for my girls even if I died. When I received the citizenship, my eyes were strained, I was exhausted from being so very sick but I held this paper in my hand and remembered Philippians 3:20 which says this earth is not my home but my true citizenship is in Heaven. As happy as I was to become an American citizen and thankful, I still knew where my true hope lay and that it is in eternity with Jesus.

That very day the cousin I grew up with, Rita, had come into town to visit me. Her baby was also in the hospital struggling with brain cancer. We looked at the paper and rejoiced together over the joy of being a citizen and said I can never die because now that I am a citizen, I have so many things I can and want to do here on this earth. We shed tears of joy and thankfulness and sadness all at the same time together. Bhima and Pavitra were also there. They are also cousins and came so many times to be with me at the hospital to encourage me, feed me and comfort me. We all rejoiced together as a family.

As precious as it is to be a citizen of a country with rights, privileges, security and borders, nothing can come close to the citizenship that is offered to those who are saved by the blood of Jesus Christ. No earthly home or country can compare to the perfect home that God is preparing for His children in Heaven. Salvation is the passport to Heaven that can't be earned. It is a free gift to anyone who believes in the Lord Jesus for salvation that through Him we are qualified for eternal citizenship.

To qualify to come to America as a citizen we had to go through a 15-month process in which we had to fill out forms, go through interviews, have background checks and medical fitness approval and we had to pass them all. To get a passport we had to have all of our records, and then to become a citizen once we arrived we had to live here for five years. To get a passport to Heaven, if we confess our sins and believe in the Lord Jesus, citizenship is immediate and free (Romans 10:9-10)!

Received official citizenship in hospital room, July 2014

LIVING UNDER LIES

Growing up, the cultural ideals of beauty and worth are skin color, height, beauty and education level. If you have dark skin or a certain shape of a nose or if you are short or uneducated you are worthless and less than in people's eyes. I was told I was ugly and had a poor social status. I believed these lies and wore an internal badge of shame. I wore this badge until I found my real identity in Christ. I didn't have an awareness of how wonderfully and intentionally I was created, that God knew me before I was born and that I was created in His image and likeness (Psalm 139). I didn't know I was lovable or loved.

I didn't know I was chosen and set apart by Him at that time. I didn't have a category for any of this beauty.

I was designed by the Potter, whose every design is beautiful and worthy (Isaiah 64:8). When I realized the truth of my worth it totally changed the way I saw myself and I decided to believe the truth and leave all of the lies behind me. I was no longer defined as worthless or my value was not based on my appearance or material possessions but valued because I am human, created by Him, for Him in His image and He says I am precious (I Samuel 16:7).

People look at the outward appearance but God looks at the inward beauty. I never felt anything close to beautiful before or worth marrying or even belonging anywhere to anyone. I didn't fit anywhere. What a wonder it was for me to see myself through God's eyes, through the perfect Holy Savior of the world who made me and knows me through and through. I rejected the message of darkness and have worked to live my life as a beautiful creation to Him, cherished, valued and worth dying for. Once I became a child of God my definition of worth completely changed.

RULES, RULES, AND MORE RULES: PRACTICE DOESN'T MAKE PERFECT IN RELIGION

In Nepali culture, most people are connected with religion, rituals and rules. I grew up celebrating so many festivals, observing so many rituals and following so many rules regarding dress, food, fasting, sacrifices etc. This culture is very beautiful on the outside, with beautiful colorful clothes and gold jewelry and finery. However, because of the light of Christ I was able to see all of this as a form of slavery, done apart from truth, in hopes of earning but never being assured of some type of security for the future.

When I was 10 I would fast once a year to a god for a good husband. I worshipped every full moon to ensure that I would get a son someday. When I got my period at 11 years old, I had to leave my uncle's home or our home and live with aunties on my father's side for 10 days. I couldn't touch anything except for my own plate and had to sleep on the floor on a mat made from hay and had to have my own blanket that no one could touch. So many illogical and unexplainable superstitions/rules to follow.

Each god in Hinduism was worshipped for different reasons, in different seasons, and for different purposes to gain blessing or to ensure a good outcome for the next life. In school in Nepal, we prayed to a female goddess because she is the god of education and intelligence and we prayed for a good brain from her. Another female goddess and a cow we worshipped for monetary blessing. We worshipped the sun and mint plants once a year. Most of the culture follow these rituals and traditions. Creations vs. a creator were worshipped.

If someone dies in a family, there is a prescribed mourning time with strict restrictions on food and clothing items. We have to do rituals for good karma for the next life to make it good along with speaking lots of chants from the priest and giving the priest many things for good karma.

I would not be able to provide this religious ritual for my family in the future when they die as I no longer believe in karma for salvation. We must have a relationship with God while we are alive because our karma can't earn true salvation. If someone is able to gain salvation by good works then that person would boast in their abilities with pride. It is not by works, rather by grace alone we have been saved (Ephesians 2:8-10). I pray for them to accept Christ before they leave this earth. Time is of the essence because once you die the chance for salvation is no longer available. Choose this day who you will serve (Joshua 24:14). This is the day of salvation. Do not put off until tomorrow what can be chosen today (2 Corinthians 6:2).

THE JOURNEY FROM RELIGION TO RELATIONSHIP

To move from religion to relationship is a serious move with inherent consequences. Breaking your family's heart, impacting their prestige, influence and social status is heart wrenching and costly. In my case, I left Hinduism and this tore my mom's heart out because she worked so hard to teach me and raise me in the way she believed was right along with my other relatives. The pressure of coming through for her to help support her status and future opportunities especially because she was widowed at a young age was intense, and I didn't take this lightly.

I never wanted to hurt my family with my decision. But because of my understanding of the Gospel and the irresistibility of Christ, I counted the cost but chose Christ.

In Matthew 16:24-26 Jesus said to His disciples, "Whoever wants to be my disciple must deny themselves and take up their cross and follow me. For whoever wants to save their life will lose it, but whoever loses their life for me will find it. What good will it be for someone to gain the whole world, yet forfeit their soul? Or what can anyone give in exchange for their soul?"

Luke 14:27, "Whoever does not carry their cross and follow me cannot be my disciple."

To move from religion to relationship is a process of disconnecting from tradition, rituals and practices that unify families. When I abandoned these, it felt to my family like I was abandoning them and rejecting what was so important to them. I could not be with them during their festivals and celebrations because I don't partake in the rituals or worship. I left 30 years of tradition and religious practices with my family and friends. The breaking away was deeply hurtful. Although I don't miss any of those former things, I do feel sad that I hurt my family. However, I discovered deeply the peace of Christ, assurance of salvation and the promise of a secure future. I had no pull back to my former beliefs.

When I was in religion, I never had peace or hope. None of the gods I worshipped could provide me with peace or security because they are just like humans, sinful. Being in relationship with the God who made me is like living with living hope, confidence in Him and His provision and faithfulness though life is often not easy. Now I can't imagine my life without my relationship with God through Christ and I don't want to. To move from religion to relationship is to relocate my eternal destination. It is assured, can't be lost, can't be earned, free to me at no cost and all because of His great love for me. Even though I left religion, my love for my family is even deeper and stronger than it was before and I pray continually for them to have a relationship with God because religion can't save us. Religion is a group of manmade rules versus eternal and real promises from the one true God. I used to believe Christianity was a religion in the past, but it is anything but. It is all about a relationship with God through His provision of His Son, our Savior and brother.

To be in religion I had to show a type of perfection to make myself "good" or "right enough" to gain something from a god. In a relationship with the Trinity, the one true God wants us to come to Him just as we are because we are washed white as snow through the sacrifice of His Son, Jesus Christ. He never remembers our sin; it is as far as the east is from the west (Hebrews 8:12, I John 1:9, Psalm 103:12, Isaiah 1:18). God created us and puts us here to have relationship with Him and to enjoy Him forever and ever. God gives us family to have relationships on earth that imitate the relationship that He offers us. He wants us to know Him and be fully willing and able to receive all that He has to offer us.

Religion is man-made, rules oriented and performance based; there is no relationship as it is all about rules and rituals. I have witnessed young people in families that chose to marry someone that was deemed untouchable because of religion, and the family cut them off. They are not welcomed in their family home because they are now defiled and will defile the home of the family. This family performed some rituals with a priest to purify their home and to finish the cutting off of the relationship to justify their religious choice.

Manmade religion always results in us feeling weary, heavily burdened, hopeless and like a failure. It does not inspire, bring joy, bring hope or make any promises of a secure and glorious future. Once people fail at 'religion', then they are done, finished, cut off. Conditional love is all you can expect or hope for with religion and when you mess up or fail then you are exiled for life. There is no opportunity for reconciliation or redemption because the "rules" have not been followed.

Religion is an impossible master and a disloyal and ultimately unloving one. Any "love" you might get is not real because it is based on performance only, not based on relational affection. God doesn't want any of us to establish any religion; He is only and all about relationship with people. He made the way for this to happen through the washing of sins by His perfect and Holy Son Jesus. He offers us to come to Him of our own will, not because we have to or because we can be "good enough", but because He loves us and wants to bless us and bring us under His protection and instruction. He seeks us, He gives us the choice, He wants us and His love and approval are not based on whether we do it "right" or whether we are good, but rather because we are His. Galatians 2:21 says that it is not by religion but by grace that we are loved and accepted. Galatians 3:11 says it is not by works or laws but rather by faith that we are saved. The righteous person will live by faith.

We don't have to strain ourselves or starve or beat ourselves to become worthy of His love. He seeks us out. He lowers Himself to us and offers Himself to us (2 Corinthians 8:9). In relationship there is no fear; we are loved because of who we are and not what we do. We can't lose God's love and we can't earn it. It is just there for us because of His goodness and faithfulness. It is free, it is unending, it is eternal and it is unconditional. All humans are created in His image and He loves all of His children the same. Red and yellow, black and white they are precious in His sight, Jesus loves the people of the world!

God doesn't live in the temples built by human hands (Acts 17:24-28) and Psalm 115:4-8 says that their idols are silver and gold, the work of human hands. They have mouths but do not speak, eyes that do not see. Ears that do not hear, noses that do not smell and hands that do not feel. Feet that do not walk nor can they utter a sound with their throats. Those who made them will be like them, so do all who trust in them.

BORN AGAIN?

When I heard about salvation and the need to be born again, I wondered like Zacchaeus in the Bible how people could re-enter their mothers' wombs to be born again and why this had to happen. What I learned from my friend Linda and in Sunday school class was that a second birth is a birth that is spiritual, a choice to follow God. God brings the first physical birth through a physical father and mother. He offers a second birth through belief in the Lord Jesus and by the washing of the blood of Jesus Christ (John 3:3). Unless a man is born again, He will not see the kingdom of God. We have a choice about spiritual birth, even though we have no choice about our physical birth. We have a free will in which we are able to choose God or not choose Him. He never forces us to choose but rather offers it to us. If a man is born once he will die twice. Flesh gives birth to flesh but the spirit gives birth to spirit (John 3:6, I Peter 1:23). For you have been born again, not of perishable seed, but of imperishable, through the living and enduring word of God.

If he is born twice, he will die only once. 2 Corinthians 5:17 says that anyone who is in Christ is a new creation; the old has passed away and the new has come.

God wants us to live in eternity while we are yet lingering here on earth. He wants us to be heavenly minded, and mindful always of eternal life. I Peter 1:3 says, "praise be to the God and Father of our Lord Jesus Christ. In His great mercy He has given us a new birth into a living hope through the resurrection of Jesus Christ from the dead."

Being born again is having new eyes. Before we accept Christ we can only see with our own limited mind and fleshly perspective which is subject to sin and unable to be righteous or holy. God takes our (hard) heart of stone and replaces it with a heart of flesh (Ezekiel 36:26). When we confess our sins and call on the name of Jesus, we receive spiritual eyes along with the Holy Spirit, our helper. His light shines into our heart and enlightens our mind with the perspective of God rather than the fallen perspective. John 3:16 says that those who receive the Son of God will never perish but have everlasting life. We become Children of God (John 1:12)! This new identity is completely different than anything a mere human can imagine.

IF GOD IS GOOD, THEN WHY IS THERE SUFFERING IN THE WORLD?

People have asked me many times why, if God is so good, does He allow suffering? Why do good people have bad things happen to them? This is a universal question of the ages. I am so thankful that I knew that this world was a broken place and in this world we will have troubles before I got cancer (John 16:33). I was less than 2 years old in Christ when I got my first cancer diagnosis. I was no longer was under the power of lies. I could reject false accusations like being told I got cancer because of bad behavior in a past life karma. I forsook the messages of my forefathers that I was being punished.

I was pressured to come back to my former belief system to be out from under some type of curse.

However, because I know the goodness of God and how He works and who He is and has been throughout eternity, I know the things being said were bankrupt and empty. In Christ I know I am loved unconditionally and am secure under the protection of His feathers (Psalm 91:4).

I am safe in His righteous hand (Isaiah 41:10). He shelters and protects me even when I suffer under the fallenness of this world.

When I was told this cancer is a curse, the Holy Spirit brought so many promises of scripture to my mind to comfort and assure me that these accusations were hollow and false. Hebrews 13:5 (I will never leave you nor forsake you). Jeremiah 29:11 (God has a plan and purpose for me). Deuteronomy 31:6 (Do not be afraid or terrified for the Lord goes with you). Isaiah 49:16 (Our name is engraved in the palm of His hand). Psalm 56:8 (God keeps the measure of our tears in a bottle). Psalm 23:4 (Even though I walk through the valley of the shadow of death you are with me). I have my dear friend Linda to thank for teaching me all of these beautiful and timely scriptures that were used in perfect timing for my needs. I didn't blame God for my suffering. I understood His character and the condition of this world (Genesis 2:27).

God gives us free will to choose life or death. Through one man came life and through the same came death into the world through the free will of man. God is not the author of sin; the world is broken and exists under the fall of humanity. Pain, sorrow, loss, injustice and disease are all the result of living under the fallenness of sin through the act of disobedience.

God allows His children to suffer because it is through suffering that trust, dependence, and a deeper understanding of Him and His word occurs. The righteous are allowed to suffer, not because He doesn't care or wants to punish us; all punishment went to Jesus on the cross. But He allows the righteous to suffer to produce a deep faith, to give a testimony to others and to be able to receive deep understanding that can't be understood outside of great suffering and pain. Suffering produces righteousness and a greater dependence on and trust in God. A righteous person may have many troubles, but the Lord delivers him from them all (Psalm 34:19). He allows suffering to prune us so that we can produce good fruit (John 15:2). Satan is here to seek, kill and destroy (John 10:10). Satan is the father of lies.

SHOCK AND AWE

On March 9th, 2022, I celebrated with my friends over a great meal and special dessert Michelle made for me. I was 7 years cancer free, and had survived 8 years since my first cancer diagnosis. My checkup was good and I was so happy to have this time to be with my family. I had started a new job at Altru Hospital as a Telemetry Tech and felt my life was getting back on track.

However, I had lingering health issues from cancer and cancer treatment and struggled with hip pain, foot and back problems and more. I was having strange pelvic pain and I felt a strange lump in my groin. I thought maybe I had a hernia in my groin as did my doctor. My friend encouraged me to go for an MRI to check it out because she told me I had my life to lose if it was something serious. So I had the MRI. I was not too concerned at this time because I had already had cancer and what could be as bad as that?

The results of the MRI were shocking and unbelievable. I was given a diagnosis of Stage 3c Ovarian Cancer. My husband had received the news first because I had my phone in another room for the day and missed the calls. He left work and came home to talk to me about this terrible news. He thought I had knowledge of this already but I did not. He told me the hospital had referred me to the Mayo Clinic and that Mayo Clinic had called him. I was so shocked that I didn't even cry. I had zero idea that someone who had cancer before was actually more at risk for developing other cancers. I had no idea I would ever be struggling once again with this horrible disease. I felt numb and dumbfounded, shocked beyond belief.

On May 19th I knew for sure that I had cancer again. The next day, with possibly our last family picture taken, tear-smeared makeup was a problem. Urgent phone calls from Mayo kept interrupting the photo session.

I waited for 2 weeks to have a teleconference with Mayo, and on June 1st we met to discuss the diagnosis, the plan of treatment and how to move forward. I had a huge surgery on June 15th in which I had many tumors and lymph nodes removed from my pelvic area. I started chemotherapy once again on July 15th with a planned course of 6 treatments in total to conclude to conclude the first week of November.

HERE WE GO AGAIN

Treatment needed to be started right away and I needed to step into this journey with my physicians and get right into it. My former leukemia would need to be monitored, as well, with this fresh cancer diagnosis. This was a lot to take in and very, very difficult to process but, at the end of the day, I remembered where my hope lies, who is in charge of my life and who I can and do trust and that is Jesus.

I thought about Job and how his deep losses came one after another. How he was accused of wrong doing but was actually a righteous man. How he refused to feel sorry for himself but, rather, kept his eyes on the Lord and trusted Him through it all (Job 1:21-22). Naked I came from my mother's womb and naked I shall return. The Lord gives and the Lord takes away, blessed be the name of the Lord. In all of this Job did not sin or charge God with wrong.

I have decided to take each day as a gift, to live my best life daily with intentionality; putting on nice clothes, eating healthy food and having special memories with friends. Every day is a gift and when I realized the depth of the journey, I realized that I wanted something to engage in that would communicate my family history, my journey to faith and from that faith, my journey with Jesus and cancer. I decided to write a book but I am not great at typing, not feeling well all the time. My friend Michelle volunteered to help me write this book and be my typist, too. We have shared much beauty in recalling my life story. I could not have done this without her. She shared that she wanted to help me in so many ways during this cancer trial because we were not connected in my first cancer journey.

EXHORTATION

God has given us a brain to observe, discern, discover and seek out truth. I really want to encourage the younger generation not to follow blindly anyone or anything. Do not live your life according to other people's expectations, demands or rules. Find out for yourself if what you believe is true and right. God shows himself in nature and in the depths of our hearts. Search this out, put Him to the test and see what you find. You need to decide for yourself what it is you believe and why you believe it. Live your life intentionally, making your own choices about how to live and what you believe FREELY.

I was also a seeker and questioning traditions and rules and at the end of this testing and discerning I came to the conclusion that He is the Truth. Rules are karma and actually make you a prisoner, a captive. Freedom is why all of us, every human, has been created and in order for us to have our freedom, we have to know the Truth. The truth will set you free (John 8:32). If we do not know the truth, we will be deceived by many lies from the enemy and the world. Seek and you will find, knock and the door will be opened to you (Matthew 7:7-8).

The world and people will promise you fame, fortune, glory, luxury and riches. It will also teach you to love money which is the root of all evil (1 Tim 6:10). You might obtain all of these but these things will never satisfy what your soul is longing for because all humans are created to be known by and loved by God. There is temporary satisfaction from worldly things but they only leave the soul craving and alone. I Timothy 6:9 says, "But those who desire to be rich fall into temptation, into a snare, into many senseless and harmful desires that plunge people into ruin and destruction." For God so loved the world that he gave his one and only son so that anyone who believes should not perish but have everlasting/eternal life (John 3:16). Do you believe God loves you? Who is the God of the Bible? Where do you go for answers?

Do you believe?

NO HUMAN IS A MISTAKE

Sometimes you hear people say that their child was an accident, or when their children do things they disapprove of they express the wish that their child had died in the womb rather than to bring shame on the parents. I have witnessed many parents say these same curses on their children who have disappointed them or let them down in some way. God has a lot to say about people because He is the creator of all humans. He makes every person intentionally and, furthermore, He makes every person with a purpose, a calling on their life. John 1:13 says we are "children born not of natural descent, nor of human decision or a husband's will, but born of God."

No person is a mistake regardless of what any other human perspective says. God has a plan for every person and He makes them in His image. He creates them to have a relationship with Him, to be loved by Him and to love Him and other people. We can't find our purpose in life outside of a relationship with Him no matter what gifts, intelligence or skills we possess. He creates all of us to glorify and honor Him with our lives using the gifts He gives us. Our worth in His eyes will never change based on our behavior. He loves His children with an everlasting love and values people because they are made in His image. His love is unconditional for those who choose Him. Isaiah 49:15 says, "Can a mother forget the baby at the breast and have no compassion on the child she has borne? Though she may forget, I will not forget you!" He says that we are engraved on the palms of His hands and no one can ever take us from Him.

DO WE COME FROM MONKEYS?

I was taught all my life growing up that humans sprouted from monkeys and that the only difference once a human forms from a monkey is that the tail is missing. I was also told in a religious belief that I became a human after going through 84 lakhs (840,000 life cycles). I really wondered where I came from and how I got to where I am today. I had no memory of being a monkey or living 840,000 lives before this one. It is hard to be told these lies and try to understand my purpose for being on earth and even more so my true worth.

I have yet to see any monkey turn into a human and from all recorded history no one has witnessed this either. God created every creature with a purpose and though some do go through transitional stages, such as a butterfly, the butterfly was always going to be a butterfly because God created it with intention and for a purpose. He doesn't create creatures and throw them into the world to transform into other creatures or humans. He is an intentional and perfect God who has a purpose for everything that He does. The Bible clearly states in Genesis that He created everything in order and with purpose according to His timing and will, starting with the sky and the stars, the oceans and the mountains and ending in His greatest and highest creation, mankind.

People are the only creation that is made in His image and He values them above all else. Genesis 2:7 says, "Then the Lord God formed a man from the dust of the ground and breathed into his nostrils the breath of life and the man became a living being." We hear about science and scientists who discover creatures, concepts and creations, but they are not the originators of these. They are discovering what God has built into creation for them to discover and, further, they discover because they are fulfilling their purpose under His will to bring new things to light in the world. We give people credit for being originators of theories or being the discoverers of creations. However, they are actually finding what God has made and created for them to find and share with humanity. He gets all the credit and all the glory because we humans are incapable of originating anything. God made it all and gives the ability for discovery.

YOU HAVE INSURANCE BUT DO YOU HAVE ASSURANCE?

In this world we go to many lengths to purchase insurance for our homes, cars, medical services and more. We see how very important and essential this is for a positive and safe outcome in this life. We work so hard to provide this assurance for our lives. All this insurance is not full coverage; even the best insurance still requires some of our own additional resources to pay the bills.

For all humans it is critical to think about not just life here on earth but about some type of insurance for life after this world. In the Bible we find the concept of "assurance." "Faith is not what we see but what we don't see" (Hebrews 11:1-3). These verses go on to say, "Now faith is confidence in what we hope for and assurance about what we do not see. This is what the ancients were commended for. By faith we understand that the universe was formed at God's command, so that what is seen was not made out of what visible."

What does it mean to have eternal assurance? It means we don't have to pay for it- not monthly, not yearly, not at all. Jesus, the Son of God paid all of this for all who believe in Him on the cross at Calvary, once for all time. Jesus had all the wealth of eternity but submitted himself to human form and became poor in order for us to become rich (2 Corinthians 8:9). If we had no health insurance for a month we would be so worried and panicked. So why is it that we don't have that same concern over our eternal "insurance"? It doesn't matter really in the end what type of earthly, perishable insurance we have on "things"; it really doesn't gain us as much as we want it to or promise us anything solid. However, heavenly insurance in the form of assurance gains for us what we can't attain for ourselves and lasts throughout all eternity and has 100% coverage!

God wants all people to have the confidence of King David in Psalm 23:6 when he says, "surely goodness and love will follow me all the days of my life, and I will dwell in the house of the Lord forever." Do you want to have a living hope? Do you want to have eternal insurance? Do you want to live peacefully, fully resting in the provision already made and paid for you?

IS THE BIBLE TRUE? PROVE IT!

The Bible is not a fairy tale or folklore or even tradition. It is the inspired word of God, written by the Holy Spirit, one of the three parts of the trinity. The Bible is the absolute, unadulterated, true word of the Trinity. It never changes, it stands on its own merits through all eternity and it is one of the three eternal things in this world. The Bible makes its claims based on eyewitnesses throughout history along with archeological support. It also connects belief to visible evidence so that we can believe with certainty (Luke 1:1-4). The Bible was written by those who saw, heard and had fellowship firsthand with Jesus. Jesus' life, death and resurrection is factual history, recorded and affirmed. I John 1:3-4 says, "We proclaim to you that we have seen and heard, so that you also may have fellowship with us. And our fellowship is with the Father and with his Son Jesus Christ." The Bible is exclusively true and is meant to be interpreted in that manner. John 17:17 says, "your word is truth."

No other person or religious leader ever died and then rose back to life in recorded history. Death had no grip on Jesus because He is the one and only Son of the Living God. The prophets of the Old Testament thought their message was most often unwelcomed and even despised, costing some of them their lives and most of them a level of rejection and contempt, never quitting proclaiming the Truth that God told them to share. So many prophets of other faiths claim deity and authority but their deaths invalidate their claims to divinity. Isaiah, Jeremiah and other prophets were mouth pieces for God, foretelling the birth and death of Jesus and also His resurrection. Jesus was seen by His followers (all who never recanted their testimony even unto terrible deaths) as documented in history after His death and burial in a tomb. Even though persecution and death came to eyewitnesses of Jesus' life and work and many attempted to banish Jesus' words, more and more people still came to faith despite this. Truth is Truth and no one can erase it because it is written on the heart of every human and it is also evident in nature, which proclaims His glory.

His life, death and resurrection are actual recorded history and supported by eyewitnesses. God can withstand any testing a human can throw at Him. He is the Truth, He is the Way and He is the King of the World. The Bible is composed of 66 separate books that echo the messages over a time span of 2000 plus years. It is consistent with itself and it can interpret itself because though human hands did the physical writing of the books, the message they wrote were divinely inspired by God Himself. Other gods that claim divinity may expect or demand people to rise up through words or sacrifices to appease them. These people hope for something good in exchange, but there is no assurance, no promise of unconditional love or acceptance, and they always fear losing approval and their eternal position.

The God of the Bible humbled Himself by coming to earth in a lowly form as a human and touched humanity through the person of Jesus Christ. Not only did He take on the humanity of flesh, leaving a perfect home in Heaven, He offered His life as a living sacrifice. He was doing His father's perfect will, being poured out daily, like a drink offering.

Jesus came to serve, not to be served. No other "deity" can make this claim. John 14:6 says that He is the way, the truth and the life. You can deny Christianity, but the denial is based on opinion only as history and facts prove its truth. Every human has the ability to know God, as He has given us an inborn thirst for Him that manifests in curiosity; though this is often mistaken in human hearts as curiosity about His creation, it is actually Him we are wired to know. Romans 1:20 says, "For since the creation of the world God's invisible qualities, His eternal power and divine nature have been clearly seen, being understood from what has been made, so that people are without excuse."

WHY SHOULD WE BELIEVE THAT GOD IS INFINITE VERSUS FINITE?

Let's start with what type of being God is. He is uncreated. That means that no one created Him or thought Him up. He is, always has been and always will be...He is the eternal one. He is also perfect, without any flaws or imperfections, every bit of His word and His will is righteous, holy and perfect. He is not in any way sinful nor is He capable of failure. He has the right to make the rules and have ultimate authority. It is because of His goodness and unfailing grace, mercy and love that He is set apart from all other human "dignities". He is the one true God because His character testifies relentlessly to His goodness. He is faithful to His word and carries out His will in a way that no one can thwart because He is the true King and ruler of the universe.

His holiness also sets him apart, as He is blameless and perfect without any weakness or flaw (I Peter 1:19). He raised Lazarus from the dead (John 11:38-44), He parted the Red Sea (Exodus 14:21), He makes the mountains smoke and He touches the earth and it trembles (Psalm 104:32). The earth trembles under the weight of His glory alone. He is the creator and sustainer of everything. Colossians 1:16-17 says, "For by Him all things were created in Heaven and on earth, visible and invisible whether thrones or dominions or authorities; all things have been created through Him and for Him."

He is by definition LOVE (I John 4:16). His love chases us down and is lavished on us, and we can't escape or deny it. His love is so powerful it is literally irresistible. He is the great forgiver because of the perfection of the covering of Jesus' blood over every sinner who wants to have a relationship with Him. His gift of eternal life is free and available to anyone who wants it.

He is the King of Kings and Lord of Lords. He rose from the dead, He is the way maker, the promise keeper and the miracle worker. What makes God is that He is unlike any human. He is above all human understanding and blameless. His will is so powerful and all-encompassing that not even a worthless little sparrow will fall to the ground and die without his permission and direction (Matthew 10:29-31). He knows us so well that every human has the hairs on his head numbered. Besides that, each star in the universe has its own name.

God is omniscient, omnipresent, omnipotent, inscrutable and infallible. He is the alpha and the omega, the beginning and the end (Revelation 1:8). God's desire is for us to allow Him through relationship and salvation by Him to change our natural born hearts of stone into soft, pliable hearts of flesh that can receive Truth and love that transforms us from the inside out into beautiful reflections of Him (Ezekiel 36:26).

EPILOGUE

I am currently neutropenic (low white blood count) so I am getting injections to stimulate bone marrow production of white blood cells to boost my immune system. I am in good spirits though sometimes in a lot of pain and always in some pain. I want to live my life daily, even though it is a struggle, and see the beauty each day brings even when it is hard. I am thankful for the treatment I am getting and hopeful that God will once again do a miracle in my life and heal me. I am grateful for my home, my family and good medical care that would never have been available in the refugee camp. I have love and support from many friends and family and am a very blessed person.

I do not want to be obsessed with my cancer, be distracted from the beauty of my life and get my eyes off of my Savior during this time. I pray, study the Word, do Bible Study and book studies with my friends and at church when I can. I listen to sermons and watch encouraging Christian movies. I have been deeply encouraged and exhorted by David Jeremiah and John Piper's sermons on why we suffer in this life. A Christian sister, Joni Eareckson Tada, is the inspiration for my cancer journey.

I am "fighting the good fight" while I fight this cancer. Also, I know God is fighting for me which is way more important than any fight I can raise (Exodus 14:14). I am not depressed and do not live in a defeated state. I feel that people who are not suffering with cancer are actually suffering more than I if they do not have a saving relationship with a loving and faithful Father in whom they can entrust their lives. In this journey I want to tell to our coming generation that suffering can come from consequences of poor choices or bad behavior but not all suffering is "earned"; that is, it is because we live in a fallen world and not from karma or from past life karma.

Currently, I have completed the six cycles of aggressive chemotherapy and the scans are looking encouraging. I will be receiving maintenance chemotherapy infusions every 3 weeks for 2 years and oral chemotherapy twice a day to prevent cancer recurrence in my abdomen, which is likely given the type of cancer I have. Though I am overwhelmed right now, I will continue to trust the Lord through this trial. He brought me through cancer twice already and so I know that I can continue to rely on Him for whatever the future holds.

Besides the struggles of life in a refugee camp for 18 years and now two separate cancers, I have been through some personal struggles which have been even worse. However, my God is bigger than any of these challenges and He is working His purposes through all these events. Looking back, one of my relatives had a retained placenta in Bhutan and, with no medical care, bled to death. However, I had a c-section for my two daughters' births, rather than dying in childbirth. I also recall as a child falling from a tree and probably breaking a rib, but I did not puncture a lung or break an arm or a leg which would render it useless. And I was never trampled by an elephant or bitten by a cobra. I can now see God's hand in all these things.

Romans 8:28, "And we know that all things work together for good to those who love Him and are called according to His purpose."

To Him be the Glory!

APPENDIX

Childhood Stories from my Life in Bhutan

SLIP AND SLIDE

Growing up in Bhutan we didn't have playground equipment or parks, games or cards. Our playground in Bhutan was the jungle (when we had to take the cattle there) and farm fields. We would come home from school in the afternoons and before we would go home, we would slide down the hills covered in the slippery pine needles. We would pile up the needles a foot deep in a long row and then sit at the top and slide to the bottom. We did this daily at least one time and sometimes more. When we would slide down, we would sometimes slide the wrong way and end up in raspberry patches with lots of thorns! I am so thankful we didn't slide into a deep ravine and get really hurt. We also used vines and thin branches as swings.

One time my cousin Rita and I were playing in the trees close to our house. She grabbed vines and I grabbed thin branches. She swung out and came to a good landing spot and returned to the top. I, however, swung out into a deep spot and landed flat on my back, knocking the wind out of me and falling unconscious! We had the normal bumps and bruises of childhood but had a very good time getting them. We had to wash our legs and arms before we went to bed each night and we always dreaded this because it would sting from all of the scrapes and scratches we got playing during the day.

We did have a playground space in the refugee camp where anyone could make soccer balls from clothes and other homemade toys. We made our own things to play with others and also to entertain ourselves. The refugee camp school had volleyball and soccer balls available for students during recess.

FEELING SNACKY

Snacks are such a big part of kids' lives here in America. There are entire pantries or containers for a variety of snacks for kids. When I grew up in Bhutan, our pantry for snacks was the orchard and the jungle. We ate many types of fruits, sugar cane and grains which we used for homemade bubble gum. However, in the refugee camp we had no snacks as there was barely enough food for meals. We had no money to buy snacks that were at the refugee camp market.

ROLLING SOAP

When I was young my cousin Rita and I were charged with the task of going to the store to get a soap ball for laundry day. We had to walk 1.5 miles one way and part of that journey was up and down a steep hill covered with pine needles to get to and from the store. We purchased the soap and on the way back home I had the soap in my hands. As I descended the hill I was running carefree, chewing the piece of gum I had been given at the store. I picked up speed and slipped on the slippery pine needles and lost my balance and the ball of soap. It rolled away into the woods and Rita and I searched and searched for it as the adults were waiting down the hill at home for us. We were so stressed that we plucked out our eyebrows, put them into our palms, spit on them and then cut them in half according to superstition. Whichever side the eyebrow goes to, that is the side we need to go to look for the soap ball. We had to leave the path and we slid on the needles and into thorny raspberry bushes as we tried so hard to find the soap ball.

We finally gave up and went back to the aunts and cousin Hari doing laundry. They always gathered at the spring where there is a huge, white stone. This is where we gathered water for drinking but also for doing our laundry. When we came back empty- handed we worried about the consequences. They were frustrated and flustered about not having soap to do the laundry so we all walked back through the woods on the trail to find the soap ball. We went to the point where I dropped it but, alas, it was nowhere to be found. It was too late in the day at this point to go back the store for soap, so they had to boil the clothes to wash them. The next time we were sent for the soap we were much more careful.

MONKEY BUSINESS

There are lots of monkeys in Bhutan. At times, during harvest and certain productive times during the farming year, we were charged with doing monkey business. Rita and I walked for an hour over this great hill to get to the farm were there was a sort of tree house without windows which provided a shade for cattle. We would stand on top of it to view all of the farm and would watch to see if we could see any monkeys. If they were there, we had collected rocks for the trip and we would yell, "Lahoy!! Lahoy!!", chucking rocks at the monkeys to chase them away until we lost our voices and send them scrambling away. Sometimes there would be a large, aggressive male monkey that would turn and chase us back but we would climb up the house and stay quiet until it left.

OVERBURDENED

Growing up in Bhutan, my cousin Rita and I as children were like sisters. We loved and enjoyed each other so much and spent lots and lots of time together. Our families had a farm over the hill on the other side from our home. Our chores and duties for the day while they were gone to the fields were many. We had to carry water one mile one way in a big pot where we got water from a pond. We had to make multiple trips to gather enough water. I carried water in a basket with a strap that went around my forehead and hung down on my back. In it I put a full water jug that we scooped out of the pond.

One day when I was walking home the strap failed and all the water came out. The pot went rolling down the sloped field. I had to walk with Rita to find the pot and repair the smashed in part.

Rita and I had to also smear the floor of our house with cow dung to make it smooth and easier to sweep and keep the dust from flying up all the time. We used red mud around the perimeter so that it looked decorative and nice. We also had to gather the poop from all the cows and bulls from the shed to put into a pit. We cut grass fresh daily for the cows to sleep on. We also had to collect the poop from the sheep and goats and put it in a pit as part of our chores. All Nepali kids had these expectations on them to make their lives as comfortable as possible while the parents are working. Rita and I were good kids who wanted to impress and please our parents.

Cooking with firewood from the jungle.

I carried water from the pond in a basket like this.

Printed in the United States
by Baker & Taylor Publisher Services